# CONTENTS

# ACKNOWLEDGMENTS

Scripture texts in this work are taken from the *New American Bible with Revised New Testament and Revised Psalms* © 1991, 1986, 1970 Confraternity of Christian Doctrine, Washington, D.C. and are used by permission of the copyright owner. All Rights Reserved. No part of the *New American Bible* may be reproduced in any form without permission in writing from the copyright owner.

Excerpt from the English translation of *The Liturgy of the Hours* © 1974, International Commission on English in the Liturgy Corporation (ICEL); excerpts from the English translation of *The Ordination of Deacons, Priests, and Bishops* © 1975, ICEL; excerpts from the English translation of *The Roman Missal* © 2010, ICEL. All rights reserved.

The excerpts on pages 94 and 95 from *Fulfilled in Your Hearing: The Homily in the Sunday Assembly* by the Bishops' Committee on Priestly Life and Ministry were copyright in 1982 by the U.S. Conference of Catholic Bishops and are used by permission. All rights reserved.

The excerpt on page 103 from *To Teach as Jesus Did: A Pastoral Message on Catholic Education* was copyright in 1973 by the U.S. Conference of Catholic Bishops and is used by permission. All Rights Reserved.

The quotations on pages 13 and 15 from *Light in the Lord: Reflections on Priesthood* by Cardinal Basil Hume O.S.B. © St Pauls 1991 are used by permission.

The permission to reproduce copyrighted materials from *Priests for the Third Millennium* and *Called to be Holy* by Archbishop Timothy M. Dolan was extended by Our Sunday Visitor, 200 Noll Plaza, Huntington, IN, 46750, 1-800-348-2440. Website: www.osv.com.

All of the papal documents quoted in this book are from the English translations as presented by the Vatican website.

# RENEWING
# THE PRIESTLY
# HEART

*Based on the Insights of*
**Archbishop Timothy M. Dolan**

## FATHER JOHN E. SASSANI

**RENEW**
INTERNATIONAL

**NIHIL OBSTAT**
Msgr. James M. Cafone, S.T.D.
Censor Librorum

**IMPRIMATUR**
Most Reverend John J. Myers, J.C.D., D.D.

Cover design by Ruth Markworth

Book design and layout by Ruth Markworth and Kathrine Forster Kuo

ISBN 978-1-935532-56-9

RENEW International
1232 George Street
Plainfield, NJ 07062-1717
Phone: 908-769-5400
Fax: 908-769-5660
www.renewintl.org

Printed and bound in the United States of America

# FOREWORD

Brothers:

It has been my honor to serve our Lord as a priest for most of my life, and more recently as a bishop and archbishop. God has blessed me with years of fulfilling assignments in service to our beloved Church. I pray that every priest can say the same.

We are priests. This is our call. This is our life.

Our mission is to minister to a broken world and to bring the person, message, invitation, and salvation of Jesus Christ to all people. People are attracted to Christ and the Church when they observe us living our vocations joyfully and zealously. Joyful living is a powerful witness. Conversely, effectiveness in living out our mission can, at times, be impeded by our occasional lack of zeal or even by our apathy. This can develop when we feel overburdened, drained, and alone.

If we are to refresh our souls and feed our zeal, we priests need to take time to be ministered to ourselves. Jesus told us where two or three gather in his name he is there among us. I believe that small communities of priests, who gather regularly to pray, discuss faith, and support one another in vocation and holiness, will experience the presence of Christ and receive insights from the Holy Spirit to better serve God's people. In these groups, we can revitalize and sustain our fraternity, which both reflects and energizes the communal life Jesus desires for the whole Church. As we pray and reflect together, we can also constantly renew our vision of our mission to lead God's people in living the Gospel by building a more just world in the work and relationships of our everyday lives.

One of the assignments that I was most fond of was my time as rector of the North American College in Rome. That chapter in my vocation allowed me to participate in the formation of many seminarians. I am pleased that many insights on priestly life from my years as rector have been integrated into *Renewing the Priestly Heart* for discussion and reflection by groups of priests today. I thank RENEW International for its innovative work in creating this helpful resource for priests. It is my prayer that these reflections will help those who are seeking to refresh their souls and renew their zeal.

To my brother priests, I thank you for all you do in service to the Lord and our beloved Church. I encourage your personal growth as you join your fellow priests as participants in *Renewing the Priestly Heart*.

God bless you.
Archbishop Timothy M. Dolan

# PRESENTING
# RENEW INTERNATIONAL

The RENEW process was first developed and implemented in the Archdiocese of Newark, New Jersey. Its success led other dioceses, in the United States and in other countries, to bring RENEW to their people and parish communities. In the three decades since its vibrant beginnings, RENEW International has touched the lives of 25 million people in over 150 dioceses in the United States and 23 countries.

RENEW International has grown organically from its original single RENEW process. Materials and training have been inculturated and made available in more than 40 languages. We have added specific pastoral outreach to campuses and to young adults. We have incorporated prison ministry and provided resources for the visually impaired.

The very core of all of these processes remains the same: to help people become better hearers and doers of the Word of God. We do this by encouraging and supporting the formation of small communities who gather prayerfully to reflect on and share the Word of God, to make better connections between faith and life, and to live their faith more concretely in family, work, and community life.

As a not-for-profit organization, our pastoral outreach is sustained in part by the sales of our publications and resources and the stipends we receive for the services provided to parishes and dioceses. However, our priority is always to serve all parishes who desire to renew their faith and build the Church, regardless of their economic situation. We have been able to fulfill this mission not only in the inner city and rural areas in the United States but also in the developing world, especially Latin America and Africa, thanks to donations and charitable funding.

As you meet in your small group, we invite you to take a few moments to imagine the great invisible network of others, here in the United States and on the other continents. They gather, as you do, in small Christian communities, around the Word of God present in the Scripture, striving to hear and act upon that Word. Please keep them in your prayer. Please also pray in thanksgiving for the many graces we have experienced and for guidance from the Holy Spirit as you explore *Renewing the Priestly Heart*.

## THE AUTHOR

Father John E. Sassani is a priest of the Archdiocese of Boston and currently serves as pastor of Our Lady Help of Christians Parish in Newton, MA. Father Sassani was born and brought up in Swampscott, MA, studied for the priesthood at St. John's Seminary in Brighton, MA, and was ordained a priest in 1980. He has served in four parishes in the archdiocese: Sacred Heart in Roslindale, St. John the Evangelist in Winthrop, St. Theresa in Sherborn and now at Our Lady Help of Christians. Fr. Sassani studied at the Pontifical Liturgical Institute in Rome and in the Christian Spirituality Program at Creighton University, Omaha, NE. He served as director of the Office of Spiritual Development in the Archdiocese of Boston from 1992 to 2006 and continues to serve as an adjunct staff member of that office, now called the Office of Worship and Spiritual Life.

# INTRODUCTION

*Renewing the Priestly Heart* emerges from RENEW International's mission of spiritual renewal in the Catholic tradition. For thirty years, this mission has been focused primarily on parish communities. *Renewing the Priestly Heart* focuses on another specific community in the Church—the presbyterate. Inspired by *Priests for the Third Millennium* by Archbishop Timothy M. Dolan of New York, *Renewing the Priestly Heart* looks at the various ministerial roles and experiences of priests as ongoing opportunities for spiritual renewal. As in the other programs offered by RENEW International, the context for spiritual growth is a small faith community. *Renewing the Priestly Heart* can be used by existing support groups for priests that are organized by priests themselves or by dioceses or religious orders seeking to provide opportunities for renewal and fraternal support. *Renewing the Priestly Heart* offers priests another means by which they can "stir into flame the gift they have received through the laying on of hands" (cf. 2 *Timothy* 1:6).

# FAITH SHARING IN A SMALL COMMUNITY

Welcome to *Renewing the Priestly Heart*

Some of you already meet or have met with small groups of priests—such as *Jesus Caritas*—for faith sharing, support, and fellowship. For others, this may be a new experience and one you may want to continue after you have completed the twelve sessions of *Renewing the Priestly Heart*.

As you come together, you are not meeting only as a discussion or study group where you talk about ideas. Rather, you gather as a group, open to the Holy Spirit, seeking to grow in faith in your priesthood and in your relationship with God and one another.

For all of you engaging in this adventure, here are some key ideas that help bring about good, healthy conversation about our faith.

## GATHERING

The first fundamental is that you have chosen to gather as a small community focusing on prayer, life, ministry, and faith in a way that will enrich your own lives and vocation, the life of your parish, and the life of the diocese as a community. The members of a small group need to get to know one another. If there are priests in your group who are not familiar with each other, allow time for introductions at the first session. At later sessions, take a few moments to ask each other how you are and what has happened since you last met. If anyone new joins the group, again allow time for introductions. The goal is to form a community.

## ENVIRONMENT

The right atmosphere is important. The members of the group need to feel comfortable, physically and psychologically. Effective participation requires a reflective atmosphere, with as few distractions as possible. It is good to establish a focus, using something, such as a Bible and a burning candle, that will help direct thoughts toward the theme of the session.

## TIMING

Under most circumstances, a session should last 90 minutes. Most groups then extend their time together in a brief social. The session should have a balance of praying, relating personal experience, exploring Scripture, reflecting, faith sharing, and talking about ways of living out faith. This balance is presented in more detail on pages xvi–xvii.

## PRAYER

Invite different members of the group to lead the moments of prayer. Silence is a very important part of any prayer, so build moments of quiet into the time of prayer, with a gentle but explicit prompt from the person leading the prayer. For example: "Let us spend a few moments in quiet, becoming more aware of God's presence, God's presence in each one of us, and especially in this community, gathered in Jesus' name." Your group might also want to consider praying *The Liturgy of the Hours* together.

## MUSIC

You may wish to include music in the sessions, perhaps singing hymns from the missalette or from *The Liturgy of the Hours*.

## SCRIPTURE

These sessions give prominence to exploring Scripture, noticing what word, phrase, or image from it speaks to us or touches our hearts. The reflection more deeply explores the Gospel story; then we reflect together on our experience, our story and God's story—and above all how the two are linked. Each person who wishes to share his reflection aloud is given the opportunity to do so. No one dominates, and no one has to talk unless he wants to.

## EXPERIENCE

Our experience is essential to our spiritual lives. We need to reflect on our story—what we have experienced in our ministry, among our fellow priests, and in our other relationships—and explore how that relates to the theme of the session. The reflections encourage us to recall our experiences and then to interpret that experience through the eyes of faith.

## CHALLENGE AND COMMITMENT

A key component of this experience is how we take what we hear and share, and live it out in our lives. That is why a moment of challenge is built into every session—an opportunity to respond, not just verbally, but by making a commitment to a specific action in our ministries or in our broader lives that we see as a consequence of living out the faith expressed in the sharing. At the following meeting, we are invited to share how we did at living out that commitment.

## ROLE OF THE FACILITATOR

The facilitator of a faith-sharing community is not someone with all the answers who is there to preach or teach. The facilitator is a participant, with the particular responsibility of helping the group by:

- preparing for each session. This involves reading over the session in advance so as to be totally at home with the focus, reflection, and questions. It could also include delegating the members who will lead the prayer and arrange the environment;

- keeping the conversation focused on the theme of the session. This means moving the sharing from one moment to another, so that the balance and timing are respected;

- listening, and being prepared to ask questions that will keep the conversation moving yet focused.

- ensuring that every participant who wants to speak has the opportunity to do so. More detailed suggestions for the facilitator are included in *Sowing Seeds: Essentials for Small Community Leaders*, which is available from RENEW International. See details on page 112.

# FAITH-SHARING PRINCIPLES AND GUIDELINES

The following guidelines will keep your community focused and help you to grow in faith, hope, and love.

## PRINCIPLES

- Faith is a gift from God. God leads each person on his or her spiritual journey. This happens in the context of the Christian community.

- Christ, the Word made flesh, is the foundation of Christian faith. It is because of Christ, and in and through him that we come together to share our faith.

- "Faith sharing" refers to the shared reflections on the action of God in one's life experience as related to Scripture and the faith of the Church.

- Faith sharing is not discussion, problem solving, nor Scripture study. It is an opportunity for an encounter between a person in the concrete circumstances of his life and a loving God, leading to a conversion of heart.

- The entire faith-sharing process is an expression of prayerful reflection.

## GUIDELINES

- Constant attention to respect, honesty, and openness for each person will assist the community's growth.

- Each person shares on the level where he feels comfortable.

- Silence is a vital part of the total process. Participants are given time to reflect before any conversation begins, and a period of comfortable silence might occur between contributions by individual participants.

- Before speaking a second time, participants are encouraged to wait until all others who wish to do so have contributed.

- The entire community is responsible for participating in the conversation about our faith.

- Confidentiality, allowing each person to speak honestly, is essential.

- The natural culmination of the faith conversation should be the action commitment, the key to the spiritual growth of both individuals and community.

# SUGGESTIONS FOR THE LEADER

You have the privilege of helping the small community gain a deeper awareness of God's dynamic presence in each member's life. Your own relationship with Jesus, through prayer, the celebration of the sacraments, and practicing your faith in ministry and in your daily life, will help you lead group members to richer prayer and transformative action.

## PREPARATION

- Make a phone call to each priest in your group to remind him of the first meeting. You may either order the faith-sharing books for the group and distribute them in advance or remind each priest to order a book on line at least a week before the first session. Invite the members to read the first session, including the Gospel passage. At the end of each session, encourage participants to prepare for the next week in the same way.

- Before the meeting, prayerfully reflect on the session. Prepare whatever is needed for prayer—such as CDs and sound equipment—or share this responsibility with another member of the group. On the day of the meeting, arrange the room for prayer and sharing.

- It would be most helpful if some or all members of the group had a Bible at the meeting.

## TIME AND ATMOSPHERE

Begin each session according to the schedule decided upon by the group. Create a relaxed atmosphere (suggestions for the environment are included). Be respectful and supportive of each member.

## CONFIDENTIALITY

Remind the group of the obligation to keep all personal conversation confidential.

## REFRESHMENTS

You may want to share a meal or serve light refreshments after each session.

# THE STRUCTURE AND FLOW OF A SESSION

The key elements of faith sharing are Gather, Reflection, and Invitation to Act. The structure is designed to provide a natural flow to a session—one part leading the participants to the next, deeper stage. Having a structured routine frees the group from having to figure out "What do we do next?" It allows the members to concentrate on the what, rather than the how, to pay more attention to their inner selves and to the Word of God.

If you follow the suggested timings, a session will last approximately 90 minutes.

## GATHER *(Step 1: 40 minutes)*

### FOCUS FOR THE SESSION

Read the aim to call to mind the focus of the session. (5 minutes)

### INTRODUCTIONS

If the group has not met before or if some participants do not know each other, an opportunity to get acquainted is important. People share most easily when they feel comfortable and accepted in a group. (5 minutes)

### INVITATION TO PRAY

Each session begins with a time of prayer. Prayer must always be at the heart of gatherings of Christians. (5 minutes)

### A LOOK BACK

The facilitator invites members to share their recent experiences, including—beginning with the second meeting—their experiences with their commitment to act. (10 minutes)

### SCRIPTURE

A member of the group proclaims the Gospel. After a few minutes of silent reflection, the facilitator asks if anyone would like to share on the passage. (15 minutes)

# REFLECTION *(Step 2: 35 minutes)*

### CONVERSATION

Each reflection begins with a personal story that can be read silently or aloud. Allow time for members to consider their individual responses before moving to the question. Allow sufficient time for all to share. (15 minutes)

The main reflection can be read aloud or silently. (5 minutes)

Allow time for members to consider their individual responses before moving to the questions. Allow sufficient time for all to share. (15 minutes)

# INVITATION TO ACT *(Step 3: 15 minutes)*

### MISSION

Each session offers some ideas for an action; however, these are only suggestions. It is important that group members choose an action that is both measurable and realistic. (10 minutes)

# INVITATION TO PRAY

The facilitator invites the members to offer spontaneous prayer for their own needs and the needs of others.

The facilitator may use the suggested closing prayer or substitute another that reflects the theme of the session. (5 minutes)

# THE IDENTITY OF THE PRIEST

"The priesthood is a call, not a career; a redefinition of self, not just a new ministry; a way of life, not a job; a state of being, not just a function; a permanent lifelong commitment, not a temporary style of service; an identity, not just a role."

—**Archbishop Timothy M. Dolan**
*Priests for the Third Millennium*, **p. 228**

## ENVIRONMENT

*A Bible and a burning candle are placed on a small table. The Bible is open to the Scripture reading for this session. Consider decorating the table in the liturgical color for this season.*

## FOCUS FOR THIS SESSION

Many people and experiences in our lives helped to form us for the priesthood. However, our identity as priests is conferred on us by God when we are ordained. From that moment on, we are one with Christ in his identity and therefore in his ministry.

## GATHER

*Facilitator:*  Welcome to *Renewing the Priestly Heart,* an opportunity to take time away from our busy lives to reflect on Scripture, deepen our prayer lives, reflect on our ministerial and personal experiences in light of our conversation, strengthen our bonds as brother priests, and become better ministers.

*The facilitator invites the group members to briefly introduce themselves to each other and briefly explain why they joined this group.*

## OPENING PRAYER

*Facilitator:* Let us pray.

**All:** **Lord Jesus, you called us, and we are following you. You chose us to work with you, and we said, "yes." Help us in our lives and our vocation as priests to bring in an abundant harvest of men, women, and children who are drawn to your Father's house, to share in the life you offer. Glory and praise to you, with the Father and the Holy Spirit, forever and ever. Amen**

## A LOOK BACK

*Facilitator:* As we gather to support one another in our renewal as priests, let's begin by talking about our present lives as men, as disciples, and as ministers.

■ What have been the moments of blessing and of challenge, of joy and of frustration, in our ministry, our prayer, and our times of leisure?

# SCRIPTURE

*The facilitator invites a member of the group to proclaim the Gospel.*

Matthew 9:35-38

*Facilitator:* Let's have a few minutes of conversation about our response to the word of God.

- What word, phrase, or image from this Scripture reading touches your heart or speaks to your life?

- How do you apply the image of shepherd to your priesthood?

## REFLECTION

A young priest I know fairly well occasionally answers the rectory telephone by saying, "Hello, St. Mary's Parish. This is John Smith." He told me that once or twice the caller happened to be his mother, who said, "You worked long and hard to get to be called 'Father,' and I think you should introduce yourself that way."

When I look back at my early years as a priest, I realize that I had to adjust more than a little bit, not only to the duties of the priesthood but also to my identity as a priest. However, many people and many circumstances helped me. I am sure the same is true for you. Our parents, ordination classmates, seminary faculty, priests in the parishes where we grew up, and the faithful Catholic people in our parish communities, all have assisted us in our formation as priests. Christ was present to you and to me through these people who helped form us for ordination and for our lives as priests. Through them, Christ was infusing his identity into each of us, both as Christian men and as Catholic priests.

The road to ordination prepared us for our identity as priests, and life after ordination has developed it. After the Litany of the Saints during the ordination liturgy, the bishop said, "Hear us, Lord our God, and pour out

"'The Spirit of the Lord is upon me' (Lk. 4:18). The Holy Spirit poured out in the sacrament of holy orders is a source of holiness and a call to sanctification. This is the case not only because it configures the priest to Christ, the head and shepherd of the Church, entrusting him with a prophetic, priestly and royal mission to be carried out in the name and person of Christ, but also because it inspires and enlivens his daily existence, enriching it with gifts and demands, virtues and incentives which are summed up in pastoral charity. This charity is a synthesis which unifies the values and virtues contained in the Gospel and likewise a power which sustains their development toward Christian perfection."

—Pope John Paul II,
*Pastores Dabo Vobis*, §27

upon this servant of yours the blessing of the Holy Spirit and the grace and power of the priesthood. In your sight we offer this man for ordination: support him with your unfailing love." I always get caught by these words: "In your sight we offer this man for ordination." The bishop does not say, "we present this man," nor does he say, "we ask that you ordain this man." No. He says, "We offer this man." It reminds me of what happened when each of us was "offered" for baptism: we became, in Christ, the sons and daughters of God. It also reminds me of what happens when the bread and wine are "offered" at the Eucharist: they become Christ's true body and blood. And all of us who received Holy Orders became people whose unique identity participates in the unique identity of Christ the Priest.

What does this mean to us in our everyday lives? Perhaps, we don't relate to it much until the phone rings in the middle of the night, until a conversation with a person deepens, until a request requires something of us or challenges us to the core, or until we come to the words in the Eucharistic Prayer: "This is my body, this is the chalice of my blood—for you." Ordination identifies us with Christ the Priest, offering himself to the Father in love and to others in saving service.

We are one with Christ in his priestly identity. When we were baptized, the Holy Spirit defined us as sons of the Father, lifelong followers of Christ, and brothers to Christ and to all the baptized. At ordination, the Spirit defined us again as men who share in Christ's priestly identity and ministry forever. Being defined by his priestly identity implies that we share in Christ's identity as the one sent into the world for the wellbeing of people—no

"We are priests; yes, the doing, the ministry, is mighty important, but it flows from the being: we can act as priests, minister as priests, function as priests, serve as priests, preach as priests, because first and foremost we are priests! Being before act! *Agere sequitur esse*, as the Scholastics expressed it. Father William Byron, the former president of The Catholic University of America, is fond of saying that 'we are human beings, not human doings, and our basic dignity and identity comes from who we are, not from what we do.' This is true as well of the priesthood."

—Archbishop Timothy M. Dolan, *Priests for the Third Millennium*, p. 228

matter what the cost, and Christ's fidelity, his faithful love of the Father for the sake of the kingdom.

The identity and the fidelity of Christ are available to the members of the Church through various channels, including the saints, lay ministries, and Christian fellowship, but they are available in a personal and sacramental way through our lives and our ministries as priests. The Church is the Sacrament of Christ in the world and, in the Church, we are the Sacrament of Christ the Priest to our brothers and sisters in faith, and to people outside the community of the Church as well.

We are called to be as faithful to our identity as Jesus was to his, and—as Archbishop Dolan reminds us—this will be more challenging at some times than at others. "Fidelity will be easy," the archbishop writes, "when our priestly lives are happy, interesting, invigorating. Ah, but the sorrow, loneliness, frustration will come, and then can we be faithful? Yes, if we know that our fidelity is not to a job, a career, a function, an assignment, but to a call, an identity, a Person, namely Jesus and his Church! It is not based on achievement, reward, or fulfillment" (*Priests for the Third Millennium*, p. 232).

Nor is it based on emotion, including the many feelings that may have swept over us at ordination. St. Camillus de Lellis, a 15th century monk who devoted himself to caring for the sick, summed it up: "Commitment is doing what you said you would do after the feeling you said it in has passed."

Christ, our model, consistently manifested his priestly identity, in his hidden life and his public life, through his death and into the Risen Life of Easter. There is never a moment when his identity isn't visibly expressed in his character. We see it:

- in his union with the Father

- in his humanity, born of the Virgin Mary

- in his attentiveness to the Spirit

- in his devotion to his disciples

- in his compassion for the poor and the marginalized

- in his clarity regarding his purpose and mission

- in his capacity for forgiveness and mercy

- in his carrying the cross, dying and being buried

- in his risen life as the source of our life

All of this expresses Christ's identity—that He is from the Father and for us. In him, we are from the Father and for others. That is our identity.

We hear something of the mystery of our priestly identity in Christ in the seventeenth chapter of St. John's Gospel—the Priestly Prayer of Jesus. Two verses, in particular, express Jesus' identity, and, therefore, our identity in him:

"As you sent me into the world, so I sent them into the world. And I consecrate myself for them, so that they also may be consecrated in truth" (*John* 17:18-19).

Jesus, as he is about to leave the world, makes an offering of himself in order to send his disciples into the world. Jesus, in speaking to the Father about his followers, certainly includes those who would become his priests in the Church. The Church often uses this Gospel passage at the Liturgy of Ordination, thus letting these words of the Lord interpret what is happening to those being ordained as priests. These words express our identity in Christ.

# CONVERSATION

*Facilitator:* Let's take a few minutes to reflect on and talk about the following questions:

■ Who are some of the people who have helped you develop your priestly identity, and how did they contribute to your self-awareness as a priest? What situations in your life have challenged you to question and deepen your identity as a priest?

■ When you were first ordained, how did you understand your priestly identity? How has that understanding matured or changed over the years?

■ Besides the Scripture texts we have considered today, are there other passages from the Scripture that help you understand yourself as a priest? If so, what impact have those Scripture passages had on your identity as a priest?

"We priests can bring out the best in one another. When we visit, share a drink, meal, day off, or vacation, discuss things, let off steam with one another, challenge one another, ask a brother if something is bothering him, or pray together, we enhance one another's priestly identity. Events such as support groups, days of prayer, study days, priests' retreats, convocations, confirmations, forty hours, deanery meetings, priests' funerals and jubilees, or just plain get-togethers—these are all good ways to build up our common identity as priests."

—**Archbishop Timothy M. Dolan,**
*Priests for the Third Millennium,* **p. 235**

## MISSION

*Jesus emphasized the connection between faith and action, between what we believe and what we do. In that spirit, decide on an individual or group action that flows from what you have talked about in this session. If you decide to act on your own, share your decision with the group. If you decide on a group action, determine among you whether individual members will take responsibility for various aspects of the action.*

*You are likely to benefit most from taking an action that arises from your own response to the session. However, if you don't sense God asking something specific of you, you can consider one of the following suggestions or use these ideas to help develop one of your own:*

- Write a note or an e-mail to a person who assisted in developing you as a priest.

- Are there ways that we might assist one another in this community in strengthening the gift of our identity as priests? If so, how might we offer you that help?

- Pray over Jesus' words in *John* 17:18-19, a passage often read in the liturgy of ordination. Ponder over them as words Jesus is speaking to us, helping us to deepen our appreciation of our vocation.

- Keep a journal of your thoughts about the gifts of priesthood as you explore them through these sessions.

## CLOSING PRAYER

*Facilitator:* Let's conclude our session in prayer:

There are so many people who have assisted us along the way, or who are in need of assistance at this moment. Let's bring them before the Lord in prayer. Please express your prayers aloud or in the silence of your hearts.

Let's gather all of our prayers together now by praying as the Lord taught us:

*All:* **Our Father …**

*Facilitator:* Lord God, strengthen us who have answered your call to priesthood so that, as we serve your people, we may always be aware that we carry out this mission in both the name and the person of your son, Our Lord Jesus Christ, who lives and reigns with you and the Holy Spirit, one God, forever and ever. Amen.

# SPIRITUALITY AND THE CATHOLIC PRIEST

"To know Jesus, to hear Jesus, to love Jesus, to trust Jesus, to obey Jesus, to share his life in the deepest fiber of our being, and then to serve him in his people—this is our goal."

—Archbishop Timothy M. Dolan
*Priests for the Third Millennium*, p. 162

## ENVIRONMENT

*A Bible and a burning candle are placed on a small table. The Bible is open to the Scripture reading for this session. Consider decorating the table in the liturgical color for this season.*

## FOCUS FOR THIS SESSION

Like Christ, priests are men who are endowed with the Holy Spirit. Like all Christians, priests are called to nurture and express our spiritual lives. Prayer, particularly *The Liturgy of the Hours*, helps us do both.

## GATHER

### OPENING PRAYER

*Facilitator:* Brothers, let us join together in prayer:

**All: Merciful God, Father of our Lord Jesus, and our Father too, help us to be men of prayer, better able to lead your people in prayer. Fill us with the Spirit, so that we may hear the voice of your Son calling us to work with him, to live for him, to pray through, with, and in him.**

**We ask these things through Christ our Lord. Amen.**

## A LOOK BACK

*Facilitator:* As we gather to support one another in our renewal as priests, let's begin by talking about our present lives as men, as disciples, and as ministers.

- What have been the moments of blessing and of challenge, of joy and of frustration, in our ministry, our prayer, and our times of leisure?

- Share briefly your experience of putting into effect the action you chose to carry out after our last meeting.

# SCRIPTURE

*The facilitator invites a member of the group to proclaim the Gospel.*

**Luke 4:16-21**

*Facilitator:* Let's take some time for conversation about our response to the word of God.

- What word, phrase, or image from this Scripture reading touches your heart or speaks to your life?

- What does it reveal to us about Jesus?

- Where do you, even in this short text, find points of contact between his life and yours, his ministry and yours?

# REFLECTION

Like all believers, we priests have to grapple with our lives of faith—with what we believe and how we believe and how the faith shapes us into being men of the Spirit. In this regard, St. James offers us good advice in his letter:

"Be doers of the word and not hearers only, deluding yourselves. For if anyone is a hearer of the word and not a doer, he is like a man who looks at his own face in a mirror. He sees himself, then goes off and promptly forgets what he looked like. But the one who peers into the perfect law of freedom and perseveres, and is not a hearer who forgets but a doer who acts, such a one shall be blessed in what he does" (*James* 1:22-25)

"(Growth) in holiness is not our accomplishment but a pure gift from God. The Lord does it, not us! One of the great heresies rampant in every seminary and rectory is Pelagianism—believing that we can earn, deserve, or achieve our salvation! Such an approach leads to discouragement on the one hand and self-righteousness or religious formalism on the other....

Holiness is a mystery. It will always elude us. The moment we think we have it made we'd better start from scratch; the moment we want to walk tall we best get down on our knees; and the minute we think we're without sin, we've just committed the biggest one!"

—**Archbishop Timothy M. Dolan,**
*Priests for the Third Millennium,* **p. 169**

Hearing and doing are at the center of our lives as Christians and as priests, as we listen to God's word and practice it in ministry. Hearing and doing are the means and the end of our spiritual lives. Hearing and doing are manifestations of the Holy Spirit working in us. And these gifts of the Spirit are active: they call us to actively choose them. We all listened to many homilies and spiritual conferences in the seminary. I am sure you'd agree that some of them were inspiring, and some were not. One statement that caught my attention during a homily in Third Theology—and has stayed with me since—is this: "Act like the person you want to become, and you will!" I found those words helpful then, and I find them helpful now. One aspect of the spiritual life, it seems to me, is to act like the men we became at baptism and the men we became at ordination. It is a matter of looking into the mirror that St. James refers to in his letter and choosing to mold the person we see according to the model set by Jesus. One way to envision priestly spirituality is watching Christ the Priest and choosing to act like him.

There are many practices that can help us with this lifelong process: regularity in spiritual direction, the sacrament of penance, spiritual reading, our daily review of life, devotion to Our Lady, and so on. But in our lives as priests, *The Liturgy of the Hours*, the Divine Office, is central.

There are times for us, as priests, when the office is a blessing beyond measure, merely an obligation, or a burden that finds us only reading the words, going through the motions. I think we all know these phases of our relationship with the office. We all know as well that we willingly committed ourselves to this practice. So what might help us pray *The Liturgy of the Hours* more beneficially? One thing that helps me is the belief that Christ is always praying for me, for you, for the worldwide Church, and for whole world—all the time. This is part of the mystery of his office as our Intercessor, our Priest before the Father. And, therefore, it is part of our identification with Christ. *The Liturgy of the Hours* allows us to participate in his prayer for the Church and the world in pockets of time throughout the day. It isn't always an easy commitment, but it is one of the promises we made to the Church on the day we were ordained. And it is one promise we make to the Church every day: "Yes, I'll pray for you tomorrow when you are having surgery." "I will certainly keep your daughter and son-in-law in my prayers." "I've noticed that you look sad, and I didn't know why, so I've kept you in my prayers." The commitment to prayer is an aspect of the ministry that Christ calls us to offer as priests. And like all aspects of our lives, it provides a way for us to grow in holiness even as we offer this service for others. One of the prefaces for weekday Mass offers us some insight into this mystery:

"As a priest, if you are going to minister to people and serve them and speak to them about God and try to bring him into their lives, you must withdraw from time to time to be alone with God in order to listen to His voice speaking to you through the Scriptures, the Sacraments and in your own heart."

—**Cardinal Basil Hume**
*Light in the Lord: Reflections on*
*Priesthood,* **p. 127**

"For, although you have no need of our praise,
yet our thanksgiving is itself your gift,
since our praises add nothing to your greatness,
but profit us for salvation,
through Christ our Lord."

*The Roman Missal,* **Common Preface IV**

Archbishop Dolan points out that the Divine Office unites us with Jesus in a particular way through the psalms that are central to all of the hours. "Christ prays especially in the psalms," the archbishop writes. "I must admit that the older I get, the more I appreciate the psalms. They cover every emotion. In the daily life of a priest, he will experience a gamut of emotions: when he grabs his breviary to snatch some moments of prayer, he may feel terribly tired, maybe angry, perhaps confused, at times discouraged or sad, other times joyful and exhilarated, then again sick or anxious. In the psalms of his office he unites with Jesus in expressing all of these emotions to the Father" (*Priests for the Third Millennium*, p. 260).

In addition to the office, the Scripture readings for Sunday Mass provide us with a rich resource. Praying with the readings during the week can inspire our homily preparation and deepen our spirituality as preachers. Reading the passages slowly, listening to what God is saying, pausing over words and phrases that particularly touch us, engaging God in a dialogue about what we've heard, can raise our consciousness of the real presence of God in our lives and ministry.

"If our attention to Mary stops with her, it is wrong. She loves being a means to an end, the end being her Son. True, genuine, orthodox veneration of Mary is always Christological."

—**Archbishop Timothy M. Dolan,**
**Priests for the Third Millennium, p. 328**

Finally, we have not only the example but also the prayers of the Virgin Mary to help us. Our Lady was completely receptive to the movement of God's grace in her life. We aren't always as free as she was to respond to the Lord, but we have her constant prayers to assist us in our lives and ministry. The example of her life in the Gospels offers us a model of availability to the promptings of grace. In St. John's Gospel, we have Mary's simple advice: "Do whatever he tells you." (*John* 2:5). Mary's advice was borne out in her own life. Her graceful heart was available to the Lord before and after the annunciation. At the foot of the cross, Mary was wordlessly full of compassion, as we so often are in hospital waiting rooms and in the bedrooms of dying parishioners, where our presence, our prayers, and our personal words make a difference. Because the Holy Spirit formed us to Christ at baptism and in our ordination, we have a relationship with his mother that is begotten by grace. And the hidden consolation Mary experienced at the resurrection of her son inspires our hope in our darkest hours. Mary is praying for us and with us all the time— something we are reminded of each night in Compline. I always take special comfort from one of the antiphons to Our Lady:

"Loving Mother of the Redeemer, gate of heaven, star of the sea, assist your people who have fallen and strive to rise again. To the wonderment of nature you bore your Creator, yet remained a virgin after as before. You who received Gabriel's joyful greeting, have pity on us poor sinners."

*The Liturgy of the Hours*, Volume 1, p. 1189

# CONVERSATION

We've gathered to support one another in our lives as priests. As we consider our spiritual lives, especially our lives of prayer, let us ponder a few questions to help us engage in a beneficial conversation:

- In the time that you have been a priest, how has your experience and practice of prayer changed and grown?

- What are the challenges you face in balancing your prayer life and your ministerial life?

- What helps you to balance these two aspects of your life as a priest?

"Prayer and preaching go together. Without prayer faith becomes a series of dull propositions to which we adhere, rather than mysteries which we explore. Without prayer, our outlook becomes too secular and materialistic in search of personal comfort. Many people listening to us do not want to know what we know, they want to know what faith means to us. It only means something to us to the degree that we are men of prayer."

—Cardinal Basil Hume
*Light in the Lord: Reflections on the Priesthood*, p. 117

- How has your commitment to *The Liturgy of the Hours* over the years affected your ministerial life?

## MISSION

*Jesus emphasized the connection between faith and action, between what we believe and what we do. In that spirit, decide on an individual or group action that flows from what you have talked about in this session. If you decide to act on your own, share your decision with the group. If you decide on a group action, determine among you whether individual members will take responsibility for various aspects of the action.*

*You are likely to benefit most from taking an action that arises from your own response to the session. However, if you don't sense God asking something specific of you, you can consider one of the following suggestions or use these ideas to help develop one of your own:*

- Consider deepening your commitment to pray *The Liturgy of the Hours* daily.

- As you consider your life at this time, what choices would assist you in sustaining your prayer? Choose one step you can put into practice now.

- Commit to praying during each week with the readings for the following Sunday's Mass—for yourself and for the people you serve.

- Identify one way in which you can make your role as a teacher of prayer even more clear such as inviting parishioners to pray *The Liturgy of the Hours* or the rosary with you or leading a workshop on *Lectio Divina*.

- In a journal or notebook, write down the intentions of those who ask you to pray for them, and pray for them daily in the Divine Office.

- Commit yourself to making a yearly retreat.

- Commit yourself to going to a spiritual director. Listen to Father Joseph Kelly's reflection on spiritual direction for priests in the audio book *Renewing the Priestly Heart* from RENEW International (see details at back of book).

# CLOSING PRAYER

*Facilitator:* Before we finish our meeting, let's take a moment to pray:

There are many people whom we know through our ministry who have grave spiritual and material needs. Whether or not we have prayed for them before, let's bring them before the Lord now in prayer and make them part of our prayer for the rest of this day. Please express your prayers aloud or in the silence of your hearts.

*Time for spontaneous prayers of intercession.*

*Facilitator:* Let's gather all of our prayers together now by praying as the Lord taught us:

**All:** **Our Father ...**

*Facilitator:* Almighty Father, your Son prays without ceasing for us, for the Church, and for the world. By the inspiration of the Holy Spirit, help your ministers to continue imitating your faithfulness so that their voices may be joined with yours, and so that their petitions may be heard and answered. Amen.

# THE PRIEST AS SERVANT LEADER

"Ordination reconfigures us to Christ at the core of our being, that we are priests before God and his Church, that priesthood is forever and faithful, that what we do as priests must flow from who we are, from our priestly identity. Now let's take the next logical step: our priestly identity is not some cozy, comfortable possession we keep to ourselves and hold over others. It is a gift, an identity, all right, but one that by its nature constantly compels us to selfless, sacrificial love and service to God's people!"

—**Archbishop Timothy M. Dolan**
*Priests for the Third Millennium*, **p. 282**

## ENVIRONMENT

*A Bible and a burning candle are placed on a small table. The Bible is open to the Scripture reading for this session. Consider decorating the table in the liturgical color for this season.*

## FOCUS FOR THIS SESSION

Priests stand in the place of Christ as servants. This identification with Christ affects every aspect of the priest's life. This aspect of priestly life and ministry must be nurtured and deepened as an essential quality of leadership in the Church.

## GATHER

### OPENING PRAYER

*Facilitator:* As we gather today, let's ask the Lord to continue to fashion our hearts into the hearts of men who can offer service in Christ's name and by his grace.

*All:* **O God, you have called us to serve your people by being for them the visible presence of Jesus Christ, who came into the world not to be served but to serve. May we always keep our focus on his example as we lead our congregations in liturgy, prayer, and charity. We ask this through Christ our Lord. Amen.**

## A LOOK BACK

*Facilitator:* As we gather to support one another in our renewal as priests, let's begin by talking about our present lives as men, as disciples, and as ministers.

- What have been the moments of blessing and of challenge, of joy and of frustration, in our ministry, our prayer, and our times of leisure since we last met?

- Share briefly your experience of putting into effect the action you chose to carry out after our last meeting.

# SCRIPTURE

*The facilitator invites a member of the group to proclaim the Gospel.*

John 13:1-5, 12-15

*Facilitator:* Let's have a few minutes of conversation about our response to the word of God.

- What word, phrase, or image from this Scripture reading touches your heart or speaks to your life?

- How can the "model" Jesus presents in this passage be reflected in our ministry?

- What does this passage imply for our relationships with each other and with our parishioners?

## REFLECTION

One year, as Holy Week was approaching, my pastor asked me to assemble twelve people for the washing of the feet. He advised me to have as diverse a group as possible. I am a procrastinator, so by Tuesday of Holy Week I had only eight people. I decided to call married couples so that I might get two pairs of feet with one call. The first couple I called were folks I had met only a few months earlier. The husband, Jim, answered the phone, so I asked him first. He said: "Sure, Father, I'd be happy to have my feet washed!" Then, I asked if I could speak to his wife, Vivian, but when she heard my request she answered, "No way!" Pleading desperation, I asked her again. "Not on your life," she replied. "I think feet are disgusting. I could never let you wash my feet, and I could never wash the feet of anyone else!" A few hours later, however, Vivian called me back and told me that, reluctantly, she would have her feet washed. I got all twelve people, and Holy Thursday went off perfectly. A few months later, Vivian asked me to pray for her elderly aunt who would have hernia surgery that week. I assured her that I would. At Sunday Mass a week later, I asked Vivian about her aunt. She told me that the surgery had gone fine, and that she had visited her aunt before coming to church. "As I was getting ready to leave," Vivian said, "my aunt asked me to help her put on her socks and shoes. So I helped with her socks and shoes and left to come to Mass." I said, "Vivian, I thought you said feet are disgusting!" She smiled and said, "I thought of all of that, but I realized Christ wanted me to do this for my aunt!"

"In our Christian understanding there is this humility before God, and then there is a humility before others—to put others first, to battle egotism, to shun honor, acclaim, and attention, to rejoice when others are preferred over us. This humility before God and others is one of the toughest virtues to cultivate but crucially necessary for the priest."

—**Archbishop Timothy M. Dolan,**
*Priests for the Third Millennium,*
pp. 54-55

We hear a lot today about "service providers." Wikipedia defines a service provider as an entity that provides services to another entity—such as a company that provides Internet access to other companies or individuals. We may be grateful that, in commissioning his disciples, Christ didn't call them "service providers" but rather "servants" who are able to know the mind of their Master, which enables them to become friends of his as well (cf. *John* 15:15). Vivian wasn't a service provider to her aunt; she was her aunt's servant and Christ's servant too. Though the word has varied shades of meaning, servants are people who put themselves at the disposal of others. It isn't just about doing the job, nor is it just about the toll it takes. Being a servant is having a relationship with another person. For us, as Christians and as priests, it's about a relationship of service to Christ and of service to his people because of the service Christ has rendered to us. His service has many facets, but it is one great action—his life, ministry, death, resurrection, and ascension, and his leadership of the Church. Christ is both the servant and the leader; these two aspects of his life and ministry are inseparable in him and they are intended to be inseparable in us, because, by ordination, we have been conformed to his image.

The leadership we offer as priests is the service we have been called to provide to the people that Christ and the Church have entrusted to our care. This service has many manifestations: parish work, teaching, preaching, care for the poor, administration, organization of

"A parish priest has a love for souls. He sees beyond bodies, good looks, clothes, defense mechanisms, social status, external appearances—and gazes at the soul. He develops a sixth sense that allows him to detect those in spiritual distress. And he has favorites, whom he searches out and spends time with: those whose souls are dark due to ignorance or doubt, and who thirst for the light of Christ, and the teaching of his Church; those of the poor, whose souls are particularly cherished by him 'who had nowhere to lay his head;' children, whose souls are so tender and eager to be properly formed; those who are sick and whose souls are heavy with pain and that piercing question, 'Why?'; those whose souls are wounded by sin or by having drifted from the faith; souls empty and fallow, sated by the lust and luxury of our age; the souls of the elderly and forgotten, which bounce to life when someone bothers to stop and chat and show interest. These are his favorites."

—**Archbishop Timothy M. Dolan,**
*Priests for the Third Millennium*, **p. 273**

ministries, and so on. However, every ministry puts us into personal contact with Christ's people. We are called to lead them, and we are challenged to lead them as their servants. This is one of the distinguishing dimensions of Christ's priesthood and of our priestly leadership.

"The essential content of this pastoral charity is the gift of self, the total gift of self to the Church, following the example of Christ. 'Pastoral charity is the virtue by which we imitate Christ in his self-giving and service. It is not just what we do, but our gift of self, which manifests Christ's love for his flock. Pastoral charity determines our way of thinking and acting, our way of relating to people. It makes special demands on us.'"

—**Pope John Paul II,**
*Pastores Dabo Vobis*, §23

Years ago, I attended a Cursillo weekend that included a talk on leaders. A speaker on that weekend defined a leader as someone who, by his or her person and conduct, influences the thoughts and actions of other people. Christ is that kind of leader. We are called to be leaders in that sense too. Many things contributed to Christ having that kind of influence in the lives of people during his public life and ministry. Sent by the Father and endowed by the Holy Spirit with an abundance of gifts, he knew himself, he understood his mission, he was filled with the desire to serve those to whom he had been sent, and he was committed to accomplishing his mission without counting the cost. His willingness to do whatever it would take to save us and set us free is what makes him a servant leader. St. Paul experienced the life-changing service of Christ. The risen Christ initiated a relationship with Saul—as Paul was known before his conversion—that led to baptism, when Christ became his leader, lord, and master. Years later, Paul was able to express something of the depth of Christ's grace that had changed his life, beginning on the Road to Damascus:

> "Have among yourselves the same attitude
> that is also yours in Christ Jesus,
> Who, though he was in the form of God,
> did not regard equality with God
> something to be grasped.
>
> Rather, he emptied himself,
> taking the form of a slave,

coming in human likeness;
and found human in appearance,
he humbled himself,
becoming obedient to death, even death on a cross"

*Philippians* 2:5-8

Ultimately, the grace that Christ offered to Paul changed *him* into a leader in the Christian community. Because of his experience, Paul understood the central characteristic of being a leader in the service of Christ. He expressed it in these words:

"For we do not preach ourselves but Jesus Christ as Lord, and ourselves as your slaves for the sake of Jesus" (2 *Corinthians* 4:5).

Saul, who cherished his freedom as a Roman citizen, became Paul the slave, the servant, because of his life-changing encounter with Jesus Christ. Something similar has happened to us.

Among the many attributes that should be second nature to us, two that are particularly fitting both to servants of Christ and leaders in the Church are humility and courtesy. The passage from the Letter to the Philippians certainly expresses Christ's humility and the call that we have to embody that selfless love in our lives. I would also say that real servants are courteous. As Archbishop Dolan indicated in *Priests for the Third Millennium*, courtesy is composed of three elements: first, self-respect; second, respect for others, and finally, civility, or consideration, or care. Courtesy is a deferential attitude toward those who need our service. Courtesy is manifested when we graciously and consistently put the needs and concerns of others ahead of our own (cf. *Priests of the Third Millennium*, p. 90). These characteristics are poignantly and clearly present in Christ's personality. For us to be formed in his image as servant leaders, we must desire to be like him and be given the grace to make the choices that will deepen our own character as courteous and humble followers of Christ and servant leaders of the servants of God.

# CONVERSATION

We can now offer a service to one another through our helpful thoughts about these questions:

- Who are some of the servant leaders in your own life, and how has their witness helped you follow Christ more generously?

- What have you found helpful about the phrase "servant leaders" and what do you find challenging about the phrase?

- How do you distinguish between overwork or tiredness and self-emptying love?

- Who assists you in sustaining an attitude of service? What practices enable you to offer servant leadership as a priest?

## MISSION

*Jesus emphasized the connection between faith and action, between what we believe and what we do. In that spirit, decide on an individual or group action that flows from what you have talked about in this session. If you decide to act on your own, share your decision with the group. If you decide on a group action, determine among you whether individual members will take responsibility for various aspects of the action.*

*You are likely to benefit most from taking an action that arises from your own response to the session. However, if you don't sense God asking something specific of you, you can consider one of the following suggestions or use these ideas to help develop one of your own:*

- Among the people you serve, who offers you a consistent witness of Christ-like generosity in the circle of your ministerial life? Make a point of expressing your gratitude to them for the witness of their lives.

- Write a journal entry after reflecting on these questions: What structures assist you in offering servant leadership in your ministry? How do these structures assist you?

- Do all the ministers in your parish or ministry have opportunities for faith formation? If not, what might you do to change that situation? Consider inviting speakers or sending ministers to continuing education programs, conferences, or retreats.

- Listen to Father Joseph Kerrigan's reflection on social justice today and the priesthood and Sister Theresa Rickard's reflection on priests and the new evangelization, in the audio book *Renewing the Priestly Heart* from RENEW International (see details at back of book).

## CLOSING PRAYER

*Facilitator:* Before we finish our meeting, let's take a moment to pray in silence:

*All:* **Almighty God, your Son came into the world to serve you by serving your people. May we follow his example by leading our brothers and sisters in prayer and in ministry, encouraging their initiative and applauding their efforts. Help us to be aware of the needs, questions, and vulnerabilities of your people and to respond to them with humility and kindness. We ask this through Jesus Christ, our Lord, who lives and reigns with you and the Holy Spirit, one God, forever and ever. Amen.**

# THE PRIEST AS COMMUNITY BUILDER

"The parish priesthood needs no recluses, no more priests who run away from people, or hide in their rooms, or in the sacristy, or become addicted to their TV or computer. Even hardworking affable guys these days can let the crush of meetings, committees, programs, or projects keep them locked inside bureaucracy, aloof from most of the people in the parish. One popular pastor told me, 'We need street priests, guys on the playground, in the homes, all around the parish, because people love to see their priest.'"

—Archbishop Timothy M. Dolan,
*Priests for the Third Millennium*, p. 276

## ENVIRONMENT

*A Bible and a burning candle are placed on a small table. The Bible is open to the Scripture reading for this session. Consider decorating the table in the liturgical color for this season.*

## FOCUS FOR THIS SESSION

Christian identity is primarily communal: The Church emerges from the communion of the Trinity, and the priesthood promotes the building up of the body of Christ.

## GATHER

### OPENING PRAYER

*Facilitator:*   As we gather today, let us ask the Holy Trinity to help us fulfill our role as builders of the Church, so that the love that binds the Father, Son, and Holy Spirit may bind us to the people we serve and, in turn, bind us all to God.

***All:*** **Holy Father, you have made us members of your Son's body in baptism and have called us to the priesthood for the wellbeing of the Church. Give us the gifts we need to build up the Church as the body of Christ in the world. Guide us and the people we serve as together we make our way to your kingdom. We ask this through Christ our Lord. Amen.**

## A LOOK BACK

*Facilitator:* As we gather to support one another in our renewal as priests, let's begin by considering our present lives as men, as disciples, and as ministers.

■ What have been the moments of blessing and of challenge, of joy and of frustration, in our ministry, our prayer, and our times of leisure since we last met?

■ Share briefly your experience of putting into effect the action you chose to carry out after our last meeting.

# SCRIPTURE

*The facilitator invites a member of the group to read the Scripture passage:*

1 Corinthians 12:3-13

*Facilitator:* Let's have a few minutes of conversation about our response to the word of God.

■ What word, phrase, or image from this Scripture reading touches your heart or speaks to your life?

- ■ The Lord has given each of us many gifts that we can use for the wellbeing of individual Christians and communities. For what gifts are you particularly grateful?

- ■ Who are the colleagues in ministry who have helped you understand the communal nature of the Church and what is needed to strengthen it?

## REFLECTION

In 1967, my uncle took his children and me to the World's Fair in Montreal, *Expo 67*. It was exciting—not only the sights and experiences associated with the World's Fair but also the adventure of being together. We were away for a week, staying in a campground near Montreal. Even at this distance in time, the memory of life in a tent is vivid—especially because it rained a lot that week. I can remember my uncle organizing us to tape the leaking canvas while he was trying to dry our socks on the kerosene lantern. That week in a tent with extended family prepared me in a small way for life in the community of the Church.

In the prologue of St. John's Gospel, we hear the poignantly rich phrase, "And the Word became flesh and made his dwelling among us" (*John* 1:14). The commentaries on the Gospel of John often indicate that the Word dwells among us as if he has "pitched a tent" in our midst. Christ comes to dwell among us, to guide us to the kingdom, and to shelter us on the way. His dwelling is the community of his body, the Church. And the tending that the Church needs, since we are undergoing a great deal of change, is not easily done.

We are keenly aware of the decline in the number of priests, the diminishing number of people participating in Sunday Liturgy, the merger of parishes into more robust communities of faith, the various forms of polarization that often reflect the polarization in the secular community, and the introduction of new ethnic groups and languages to long-established parishes. All of these things challenge us as priests to be builders and sustainers of communities. We are especially suited to do this job. We are made by the Triune God; we are created in the image of the interpersonal nature of God; we have a natural orientation toward interpersonal communion. We were born into the community of a family; we were baptized into the family of the Church. We've lived in these communities all of our lives. We are destined for community as well: the kingdom of God. The kingdom, which is the central focus of Jesus' preaching and ministry, is the community of all people and all of creation in God: the Father, Son and Holy Spirit. Communion and community truly are the beginning and the end for us.

With the understanding, then, that community is central to the Gospel and to the Christian life, what gifts do we need to help us as priests in the work of building and sustaining the community of the Church? The first gift is the firm conviction that the Church, as a community of faith, hope and love, already exists. We do not have to start from scratch. I find this a huge relief. Even if we find ourselves opening a new parish, or overseeing a merger of existing parishes, the faith communities already exist: they need to be sustained, developed, adapted, enriched, renewed, and sometimes reconciled, but we do not have to create them. Still, there will be tasks to accomplish and challenges to face in every community we serve. What other gifts do we need to bring to this ministry of sustaining communities?

"We also sacrifice time for God's people. The demands made on our time! How the priest longs for an evening alone, an afternoon without the phone or doorbell interrupting him, a day without appointments. Again, we are asked to sacrifice our time, freely to give up something we find precious for the service of God's people. This is especially true of a parish priest whose people expect his presence. Woody Allen said 'half of life is just showing up,' and that's very true of the parish priest. To be there, after Mass. at the meetings, in the classroom, in the home, at the hospital, funeral parlor, nursing home, playground, basketball game, reception, party . . . you name it. 'Father, can you come? Father, will you be there? Father, we'll be looking for you!' Priestly presence! It calls for a sacrifice of time, which can be a penance."

—**Archbishop Timothy M. Dolan,**
*Priests for the Third Millennium,*
pp. 133-134

**a. Humble availability.** As priests, we usually arrive in parishes as strangers. So we arrive as leaders who need to learn the faces, the names, the culture, the pains, the problems, the glories and successes of our communities. Archbishop Dolan points out, "A parish priest is willing to be inconvenienced ... One of the best compliments a parish priest can receive is, 'He acted like he had all the time in the world, like I was no bother whatsoever' (*Priests for the Third Millennium*, p. 275). Humble availability will allow us to serve the parishioners by slowly coming to know them as a community, to appreciate their strengths and listen with compassion to everyone who wants to be heard, including those who may seem out of step with the culture of the parish. This will really assist a leader of a particular parish who is also the "new kid on the block."

**b. Attentive compassion.** As priests, we want parishes (and other communities of the faithful) to thrive. Sometimes that requires not only new ideas but compassion. Communities suffer just as individuals do. As ministers of Christ, we need to offer compassion to communities, as well as to individuals, in order to sustain them and foster their growth. A community may have suffered the loss of a beloved priest, or changes in the neighborhood, or reconfiguration of a formerly thriving parish that has declined, or revelation of the dark side of a former pastor that has grievously hurt some and shocked others. With attentive compassion we try to attend to all of this and more, with a view to developing, sustaining, and building new levels of loving, faith-filled relationship among the people we serve.

"At all times and in every race God has given welcome to whosoever fears Him and does what is right. God, however, does not make men holy and save them merely as individuals, without bond or link between one another. Rather has it pleased Him to bring men together as one people, a people which acknowledges Him in truth and serves Him in holiness."

—*Lumen Gentium,*
*Dogmatic Constitution*
*on the Church,*§ 9

**c. Collective discernment.** As priests, no matter how much wisdom and experience we bring to a parish, we benefit enormously from the wisdom and experience of the other leaders in the community: deacons, lay ecclesial ministers, religious, directors of religious education, members of the pastoral council and finance council, parishioners who have been founding members, and the most recently registered family. The community benefits from this collective potential when we see our parishioners, and they see each other, as equal members.

Finally, since discernment is a gift of the Holy Spirit, we need to pray for the eyes to see, the ears to hear and the wisdom to decide what the Lord desires for this community, and to be guided by the lights that come from him and from his people.

As we carry out our ministry, it is important that we keep the focus on the parish as a community. Few congregations are homogenous. Much of the growth of the Catholic Church in the twenty-first century is a result of immigration, and we see that change in the faces of the people who enter our churches, pray in the pews, and receive the sacraments. It is our role to prompt the congregation to welcome newcomers, to celebrate the cultural gifts that new members can bring to a parish, and to help old and new parishioners see themselves as one and equal in the Body of Christ.

We may also encounter in our congregations differences of another kind. People who worship under the same roof may subtly or overtly distinguish themselves as conservative or liberal, as traditional or progressive, as devotees of the decrees of the Second Vatican Council or as "post council." We have witnessed in civil life the divisiveness that

"The parish is a privileged place where the faithful concretely experience the Church. Today in America as elsewhere in the world the parish is facing certain difficulties in fulfilling its mission. The parish needs to be constantly renewed on the basis of the principle that 'the parish must continue to be above all a Eucharistic community.' This principle implies that 'parishes are called to be welcoming and fraternal, places of Christian initiation, of education in and celebration of the faith, open to the full range of charisms, services and ministries, organized in a communal and responsible way, capable of utilizing existing movements of the apostolate, attentive to the cultural diversity of the people, open to pastoral projects which go beyond the individual parish, and alert to the world in which they live.'"

—Pope John Paul II
*Ecclesia in America*, § 41

can result when people are polarized to the point that they no longer recognize what they have in common as human beings. Even allowing for varied opinions, our task—through our example, preaching, and catechesis—is to encourage parishioners to respect each other's viewpoints but to see themselves as truly Catholic people with one faith and one goal: unity with God and each other.

A wise priest I know described the Christian life as "a life of high adventure." I think this life always includes risks and challenges, but it also offers rewards and blessings beyond measure, not just to ourselves as leaders but to the communities we serve. As we stand at the altar, day in and day out, we celebrate the mystery that empowers us to sustain and develop the community of the Church:

"Therefore, as we celebrate
the memorial of his Death and Resurrection,
we offer you, Lord,
the Bread of life and the Chalice of salvation,
giving thanks that you have held us worthy
to be in your presence and minister to you.

"Humbly we pray
that, partaking of the Body and Blood of Christ,
we may be gathered into one by the Holy Spirit."

*The Roman Missal*, **Eucharistic Prayer II**

# CONVERSATION

*Facilitator:* Having considered our priestly task to be builders and sustainers of faith communities, let's take a moment to reflect on what this aspect of our ministry requires of us and all that we bring to this dimension of priestly leadership.

- Having read these reflections, and mindful of your own gifts and talents, what gives you a sense of encouragement in your vocation as a priest and as a man who is called to be leader in a community of faith?

■ Archbishop Dolan describes the gifts of "humble availability, attentive compassion and collective discernment" as practical ways of sustaining and building up the Body of Christ. How might these gifts assist you where you minister?

■ How do you see polarity or divisiveness manifested in your parish community? How can you be a bridge builder between diverse groups in the parish?

## MISSION

*Jesus emphasized the connection between faith and action, between what we believe and what we do. In that spirit, decide on an individual or group action that flows from what you have talked about in this session. If you decide to act on your own, share your decision with the group. If you decide on a group action, determine among you whether individual members will take responsibility for various aspects of the action.*

*You are likely to benefit most from taking an action that arises from your own response to the session. However, if you don't sense God asking something specific of you, you can consider one of the following suggestions or use these ideas to help develop one of your own:*

■ If you haven't done this, host a quarterly welcome luncheon for new parishioners after your final Sunday Mass. Invite the staff and ministry leaders to attend. Make efforts to integrate newcomers into parish ministries and activities.

■ Everyone has gifts waiting to be shared. Consider polling every parish person above confirmation age about unique ways they can share their special gifts in stewardship to serve your community at least once each year. (This might include invoking personal talents, or vocational / professional skills, or gifted personalities, cooking, driving, etc.)

- Initiate a bi-annual parish ministry fair or an annual parish picnic on the feast day of your parish saint to strengthen and build community among your parish community.

- The theme song of the TV show *Cheers* told us that people want to go where everybody knows their name. Most parishioners know the name of their parish priest. Make efforts each week to learn the name of at least one parishioner and learn one thing about that person.

- Listen to the reflections on priests as collaborators in ministry by Bishop Robert Lynch of the Diocese of St. Petersburg and by Brother Loughlan Sofield; the reflection on the priest and the deacon by Deacon John Dumschat, and the reflection on welcoming international priests by Father Abraham Orapankal, in the audio book *Renewing the Priestly Heart* from RENEW International (see details at back of book).

## CLOSING PRAYER

*Facilitator:* Before we conclude our meeting, let's take a moment to pray:

*Moment of silence*

*Prayed alternately by two groups:*

*Group 1:* Lord Jesus Christ, this was your constant prayer for your followers: "that they might be one."

*Group 2:* You invited them to be one with each other and with you in the sacrament of your Body and Blood.

*Group 1:*   Now the care of your followers, the Body of Christ, has been entrusted to us in the parish communities of your Church.

*Group 2:*   Help us to devote our energy, time, and compassion to helping your Body grow and thrive and to encourage solidarity beyond the limits of our own interests or the walls of our churches.

*Facilitator:*   Let us pray together in the words our Savior gave us.

**All:**   **Our Father. . . .**

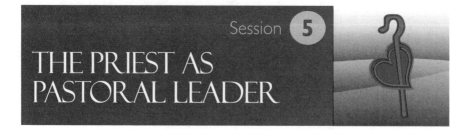

# THE PRIEST AS PASTORAL LEADER

"Priestly zeal prompts us to be self-starters, not passive, tepid men waiting for people to tell us what to do but self-starters who never find an end to their work. The days of waiting in a rectory for people to come knocking on our door seeking us out are over—we now have to go after them, and that takes zeal."

—Archbishop Timothy M. Dolan,
*Priests for the Third Millennium*, p. 288

## ENVIRONMENT

*A Bible and a burning candle are placed on a small table. The Bible is open to the Scripture reading for this session. Consider decorating the table in the liturgical color for this season.*

## FOCUS FOR THIS SESSION

The Lord Jesus established a style of leadership that is pastoral, that is, influenced by the sheep herders in his day. This style led him to describe himself as the Good Shepherd, and his style also set the tone and goal for our pastoral leadership as priests.

## GATHER

### OPENING PRAYER

*Facilitator:* Let's recall, once again, that the outward work of pastoral leadership requires an interior discipline, the discipline of being a disciple, a student, a follower of Christ. And in that spirit, let's turn to the Lord in prayer.

*All:*  **Lord God, Father of our Lord Jesus, hear our prayer. Enable us to focus our attention on him and give us the courage to follow where he leads. Help us to hear the sound of his voice, so that we will never go astray. May our choice to follow him help us lead his people. May our attention to his word enable us to issue his call to other men and women. Help us appreciate the gifts of our faith and our vocation, so that our ministry will build up your people in faith, in hope and in love. We confidently ask these things of you because of our relationship with your Son, who lives and reigns, forever and ever. Amen.**

## A LOOK BACK

*Facilitator:*  As we gather to support one another in our renewal as priests, let's begin by talking about our present lives as men, as disciples, and as ministers.

- What have been the moments of blessing and of challenge, of joy and of frustration, in our ministry, our prayer, and our times of leisure?

- Share briefly your experience of putting into effect the action you chose to carry out after our last meeting.

# SCRIPTURE

*The facilitator invites a member of the group to proclaim the Gospel.*

John 10:1-4, 14-15

*Facilitator:* Let's have a few minutes of conversation about our response to the word of God.

- What word, phrase, or image from this Scripture reading touches your heart or speaks to your life?

- What responsibilities does this reading imply for us as priests?

- How can we create in the congregations the sense of confidence the sheep have in their shepherd?

# REFLECTION

When I was newly ordained, I was sent to a large urban parish where I was the fourth priest assigned and where two others—a retired pastor and a priest therapist—were in residence. I had never imagined serving in the city or in so large a parish. It would be an understatement to say that it took some getting used to. However, four years later, as that assignment was coming to an end, I realized that it had been a providential experience. I had been living with an excellent priest who provided me with a great example of what it meant to be not only an able administrator of an enormous community of people but also a fine pastor who set the standard for all of us in that community. It would be years before I would become the administrator of a parish community, but he had already been a model for me of true pastoral leadership.

Thirty years later, I am the pastor of a large suburban parish. I have benefited from serving in five parishes so far—as parochial vicar in three of them and as pastor in two. One experience built on another. I have learned that being a parish priest, a pastor of a community of faith, requires the kind of leadership that a shepherd gives.

I have no experience with tending sheep, unless you count taking my nephews and niece to the petting zoo when they were children. But, if what the Scripture and the commentaries say accurately describes shepherding, we can begin to develop a job description.

A shepherd, a pastor, is someone who is out in front, which lets him show the way to others and do it with gentle but determined conviction. He does not come from behind and push; rather, from his place in front he takes the lead and sets the pace. He has a clear voice that manifests not only personal care for those who hear but also a willingness to do whatever is needed to care for those entrusted to him. The shepherd, the pastor, is someone who can manage with calm authority the fears of those he leads. And, the shepherd will always have an eye out for the weak and be willing, if necessary, to carry them.

None of this is to suggest that the pastor of a community is a one-man band, even, or especially, if he's the only priest in the parish or in a cluster of parishes. The kind of leadership that Christ offered was not only direct, but also indirect; his was not solitary action but communal action. Jesus was the focal point but not the only worker. His apostles had an important share in announcing the kingdom of God. The apostles worked with Jesus, by his desire and call. They drew others in, and the community of disciples grew to the point that, within only a few years, it needed a defined group of leaders in the works of service, the deacons, so that the apostles could focus on the ministry of the word. From the beginning, Christ, in his wisdom, empowered pastoral leaders to preserve and preach the Gospel and, at the same time, respond with wisdom and creativity to the growth and changing needs of the Church. He said, "Then every scribe who has been instructed in the kingdom of heaven is like the head of a household who

> "The parish priest is on the front lines of the Church. We can talk about all the programs, all the movements, all the initiatives, all the goals; we can talk about evangelization till we're hoarse, and none of these things amount to a plate of polenta if they are not implemented in the parish, led by the holy and zealous priests. No wonder Pope John [XXIII] said that being a parish priest is 'the greatest priestly work of all!'"
>
> —**Archbishop Timothy M. Dolan,**
> *Priests for the Third Millennium,*
> **pp. 267-268**

brings from his storeroom both the new and the old" (*Matthew* 13:52). And so, an effective pastor raises up other leaders from the parish staff and from the congregation, and he works in collaboration with them—empowering staff members, women, lay ecclesial ministers, and religious. It is especially important that we priests encourage women, who do not participate in ordained ministry, to share fully in the leadership and labor of the parish community. Archbishop Dolan goes so far as to write that a seminarian should reconsider his vocation if, among other things, he is "uncomfortable around women, unable to enjoy their company and collaborate with them as equals" (*Priests for the Third Millennium*, p. 312). The effective pastor also recognizes that the deacon has more than a liturgical role and encourages him to share the leadership and the labor of charity and religious education. Ultimately, the pastor shares leadership but also sees to it that the various ministries of the parish are successfully carried out.

"Not long ago, I had a visitor from my first parish assignment. I could hardly recall her. She proceeds to show me the picture of her two-year-old grandson, and tells me that his name is 'Timothy Michael,' after me, because her daughter, the little boy's mother, remembered me so gratefully from a very difficult time when she was in seventh grade. I can't even remember who she was! I never even knew I had done anything! There's the power of parish priesthood."

—**Archbishop Timothy M. Dolan,** *Priests for the Third Millennium,* **p. 279**

None of this comes easily, and some of it comes at a great cost. Therefore, pastoral leaders must be people who can approach life with both zeal and prudence. Zeal with respect to our vocation, according to Timothy, "means priests on fire with love for God and his people, priests whose greatest privilege is to serve their people, at the cost of sacrifice and even maybe life itself" (*Priests for the Third Millennium*, p. 283). But for those who hope to be effective and durable leaders, the archbishop adds a caveat: "We live a very hectic and demanding life with spiritual, academic, apostolic, community, and hospitality demands. To learn to balance them with a sense of prudence and proportion will be perhaps one of the most valuable lessons you can imbibe" (*Priests for the Third Millennium*, p. 73). Christ calls us to imitate him. As leaders in the pastoral care of his people, let's strive for the gifts we need, especially zeal and prudence, so that we can serve the Church effectively, and for the long haul, because these two gifts have shaped the nature of our leadership.

# CONVERSATION

*Facilitator:* Take a moment to consider and talk about what we have heard today—the challenges of offering pastoral leadership in the Church in our time.

■ Who are the people you rely upon in pastoral leadership in your parish—and what makes them reliable? How do they assist you in your pastoral responsibility? How do you build up their ministry as leaders?

■ When you consider your life and ministry as a priest, and your gifts as a Christian, how do prudence and zeal contribute to your leadership in your community? In what ways could prudence and zeal help you grow and develop?

## MISSION

*Jesus emphasized the connection between faith and action, between what we believe and what we do. In that spirit, decide on an individual or group action that flows from what you have talked about in this session.*

*If you decide to act on your own, share your decision with the group. If you decide on a group action, determine among you whether individual members will take responsibility for various aspects of the action.*

"Jesus is the promised good shepherd (cf. *Ez.* 34), who knows each one of his sheep, who offers his life for them and who wishes to gather them together as one flock with one shepherd (cf. *Jn.* 10:11-16). He is the shepherd who has come 'not to be served but to serve' (*Mt.* 20:28), who in the paschal action of the washing of the feet (cf. *Jn.* 13:1-20) leaves to his disciples a model of service to one another and who freely offers himself as the 'innocent lamb' sacrificed for our redemption (cf. *Jn.* 1:36; *Rv.* 5:6, 12)."

—**Pope John Paul II**
*Pastores Dabo Vobis*, §13

*You are likely to benefit most from taking an action that arises from your own response to the session. However, if you don't sense God asking something specific of you, you can consider one of the following suggestions or use these ideas to help develop one of your own:*

- Write a journal entry about aspects of your personality and priestly identity, such as prudence and zeal, that have made you an effective leader and areas in your personality that need further development in order for you to continue to grow as a leader in the Church.

- If you have a staff, meet with them weekly to pray together and to empower them to minister more effectively.

- Conduct a survey to hear from the people what they want from their parish.

- Listen to Father Robert Stagg's reflection on pastoral leadership in the audio book *Renewing the Priestly Heart* from RENEW International (see details at back of book).

## CLOSING PRAYER

*Facilitator:* St. Mark tells us that Jesus was filled with compassion for the people who appeared to him as sheep without a shepherd. Let's pray together that God will continue to give us the strength and skill to shepherd his people in the Church.

*All:* **Almighty God, give us the will, the energy, and the wisdom to lead your people as they seek to serve you in this world and to live in union with you in the world to come. Give us the strength to keep them on the path that leads to you, and the vision to see the shepherds among them and share**

**with them the care of your Church. We ask this through the Good Shepherd, Christ our Lord. Amen.**

# THE PRIEST AND ONGOING HUMAN FORMATION

"I thought of this whole issue of human formation recently while reading St. Paul. Paul is writing to Timothy about the qualities of an ordained minister, pointing out that he must be irreproachable, even-tempered, self-controlled, modest, hospitable. He should be a good teacher. He must not be addicted to drink. He ought not to be contentious; rather, he should be gentle, a man of peace. Nor can he love money. He must be a good manager of his own affairs, for if a man does not know how to handle his own responsibilities, how can he care for the Church? He must be well thought of to ensure that he does not bring disgrace to the Church. As you can see, the Church has been concerned about human formation from the earliest days."

—**Archbishop Timothy M. Dolan,**
*Priests for the Third Millennium,* **p. 159**

## ENVIRONMENT

*A Bible and a burning candle are placed on a small table. The Bible is open to the Scripture reading for this session. Consider decorating the table in the liturgical color for this season.*

## FOCUS FOR THIS SESSION

As a Christian and as a presbyter, the priest is first and foremost a man, a human being with the same dignity and the same foibles as every other person. Therefore, as priests, we must attend to our growth as human beings. Our ongoing human formation is intimately related to our lives of faith and priestly service.

# GATHER

## OPENING PRAYER

*Facilitator:* In these sessions, we are assisting one another to greater maturity as people, as believers, and as priests. But this assistance isn't simply a gift we give to one another; it is also the work of grace in us. Gathered in the Lord's grace, let us spend a moment in quiet prayer.

*Pause*

**All:** **Father, source of all life, in the ways of your providence you have led us to Christ. In him we are able to discern the blessing of your will; in him we already participate in the new humanity he offers all people. By the grace of the Holy Spirit, help us to grow and mature as men, as Christians, and as priests. May we find all we need and want in him, who lives and reigns with you and the Holy Spirit, one God, forever and ever. Amen.**

## A LOOK BACK

*Facilitator:* As we gather to support one another in our renewal as priests, let's begin by considering our present lives as men, as disciples, and as ministers.

- What have been the moments of blessing and of challenge, of joy and of frustration, in our ministry, our prayer, and our times of leisure since we last met?

- Share briefly your experience of putting into effect the action you chose to carry out after our last meeting.

# SCRIPTURE

*The facilitator invites a member of the group to read the Scripture passage.*

**Ephesians 4:1-7, 11-16**

*Facilitator:*   Let's have a few minutes of conversation about our response to the word of God.

- What word, phrase, or image from this Scripture reading touches your heart or speaks to your life?

- How do you apply to yourself St. Paul's call to "live a life worthy of the call you have received"?

- What gifts that God has given you can you nurture and develop to advance the unity of the Church?

# REFLECTION

I don't know when I became aware that I am an introvert. Officially, it may have been when I got the results of the Myers Briggs Type Indicator. I took the Myers Briggs when I was assigned to the Office of Spiritual Development in my diocese. We were a team of seven people—three lay women, two sisters, and two priests. We offered parish missions, weekend retreats, and spiritual direction. It was a wonderful assignment that enriched me personally and spiritually. At some point, we decided it would be beneficial for us to know our Meyers Briggs indicators. When the results came back, there it was: I was an "I," as in introvert. Until then, I had thought that I was shy, so learning that I was an introvert was not shocking. When I was a young priest, my shyness was a bit of a hindrance to my ministry. Wedding receptions were especially tough, since I often knew only the bride and groom. After thirty years as a priest, I am still an introvert, but I am much less shy than I used to be. I consider this minor transformation to be a manifestation of ongoing human formation.

Experience changes us. It always invites, and sometimes it demands, that we accommodate ourselves to life and its expectations of us. Wedding receptions, meetings with parish groups, encounters with disgruntled colleagues or employees, call us to use our personalities to the fullest. Sitting with people in their grief, chatting with parents about their children, offering advice to married couples who are facing interpersonal difficulties, requires not only pastoral wisdom but also the human skills and humane traits that make us more effective disciples of Christ, whose humanity was impeccable.

Ours, however, is not. I get tired, angry, and jealous. I can be timid with some and overbearing with others. I like the appearance of serenity, but I am occasionally tense. However, I am still maturing. I am still becoming the man that the Lord has created me to be. This lifelong project is ongoing human formation, and it happens in many ways.

Reading, listening to music, enjoying sports, having a hobby—these are real occasions for human formation. So are relationships with dear friends whose interests are not completely like my own, who come to know me and allow me to know them in an intimate way. Such friends are gifts in themselves, but especially to priests who have made a commitment to celibate living. I do not think of marriage as a more perfect form of life than celibacy. But I do think that for married couples whose love is mature, whose commitment is intact and healthy, whose concern for each other is primary, their relationships are a primary means of human formation. My mother and father were very different from one another, and each helped the other become better because of their relationship. He tempered her direct and at times very assertive manner. She motivated him to take deliberate action in moments when he was hesitant. They brought out the best in one another. A priest and his close friends can do as much for each other.

When I entered the seminary in 1972, the *Common Rule*—known today as the Student Handbook—said that the seminary's common life was part of the formation of future priests, even when that was fulfilled through the friction that could result from rubbing shoulders in a relatively enclosed environment. My family of four included my parents and my sister. When I entered the seminary I was eighteen years old. The faculty and seminarians became my second family of origin, where I grew in wisdom and grace. My formation has continued in the priesthood thanks to the priests with whom I have lived, the religious and lay people with whom I have ministered, and the parishioners whom I have tried to serve.

"Now, courtesy is a virtue I hope needs no definition. We know it when we see it; we sure know it when we do not. It has to do with kindness, consideration, with manners, propriety, and decency. I presume it comes under charity, the supreme Christian characteristic. St. Francis observed: 'Realize, dear brother, that courtesy is actually one of the properties of God, who gives his sun and rain to the just and the unjust out of courtesy; and courtesy is the sister of charity, by which hatred is vanquished and love is cherished.'"

—**Archbishop Timothy M. Dolan,**
*Priests for the Third Millennium*, p. 90

The number of priests and seminarians has steadily decreased. Consequently, for many of us, the workload has increased, and for all of us, there are fewer brother priests to rely on for support. These factors underscore the importance of ongoing human formation. One significant aspect of that is self-care, which means that I take all the areas of my life—my spiritual, physical and psychological health—very seriously. Self care is not a synonym for "self-absorbed." I think it should be considered a synonym for "balanced." If it is, in fact, a balanced way of life, it is one real guarantor that should enable us to serve the Church for a long time. This is essential; the Church needs well rounded, healthy priests who can work with all kinds of people for the glory of God.

One of the primary products of human formation is courtesy, which simply means showing respect for others. The Gospels describe Jesus as strong, direct, and determined but also as someone who offers respect to others, even his enemies. Jesus' life is marked by courtesy. In the chapter on Human Formation in his book *Priests for the Third Millenium*, Archbishop Dolan tells two stories that deal with courtesy. They are worth repeating:

"In 1996 I was at a reception at John Cabot University to celebrate the anniversary of the *New York Times*, when a well-known journalist came up to me. I had chatted with her in the past. This time she was very intense. She said to me, 'Tell your men to be careful!' I asked her what she meant. 'Rome can teach them a lot about what's good in the Church, but it can also teach them to be nasty, mean, ambitious, backstabbing clerics.' She went on to tell me that she had attended the big Mass in honor of newly beatified Edmund Rice at St. Peter's on Monday, and when she left, it was pouring down rain. She had a deadline to meet and struggled to get a cab and had just found one, was actually opening the door to get in, when a priest pushed her aside and jumped in. She was furious. No telling how the nasty rudeness of that priest will affect her coverage of the Church in the future" (*Priests for the Third Millennium*, p.150).

> "We are ever conscious of the fact that we are a public persona in the Church. For better or worse, rightly or wrongly, we represent the Church to people. How people think of Jesus and his Church often depends on how we come across, how our human qualities are perceived. What a heavy responsibility!"
>
> —**Archbishop Timothy M. Dolan,** *Priests for the Third Millennium*, **p. 150**

Archbishop Dolan also writes about sitting next to a stranger on an airplane. The man told the archbishop that he converted to Catholicism because of an incident he witnessed involving the late Cardinal Terrence Cooke. Cardinal Cooke was at the airport, waiting in line for the shuttle. "An attendant come up and whispered to him, 'Your Eminence, follow me. I will take you to the front of the line.' 'That's very thoughtful of you and I appreciate it, but I can wait my turn,' replied the cardinal. That act of simple humility moved me so much that it sparked my interest in becoming a Catholic" (*Priests for the Third Millennium*, p. 150).

The human formation of Cardinal Cooke contributed to his character as a man and became an experience of grace for the man who saw it demonstrated. Cardinal Cooke was a model of the effects of human formation as well as the benefits it has on our effectiveness as ministers of the Gospel.

> "In our Christian understanding there is this humility before God, and then there is a humility before others—to put others first, to battle egotism, to shun honor, acclaim, and attention, to rejoice when others are preferred over us. This humility before God and others is one of the toughest virtues to cultivate but crucially necessary for the priest."
>
> —**Archbishop Timothy M. Dolan,**
> ***Priests for the Third Millennium,***
> **pp. 54-55**

With both of these anecdotes, Archbishop Dolan illustrates the fact that a well formed personality is not a gloss for a priest but a critical ingredient in his ministry—potentially the difference between attracting people to the Church or driving them away.

The archbishop writes that he has found people less likely to be alienated because of a priest's grasp of Church teaching than because he is unreliable, unapproachable, haughty, verbose, short-tempered, or sloppy.

"Our manner, our style, our personality is to attract people, not shock, scare, hurt, and alienate them," Archbishop Dolan writes. "Thus must we be aware of those traits in our character that do indeed serve as a magnet to draw people to Jesus and his Church, and constantly enhance, refine, and improve them; and thus must we candidly confront those characteristics that wound, scatter, and scandalize people, and work to purge them from our temperament. . . .

"A man might know all about the theology of marriage, but, if he's so shy that he can't introduce himself to people, he won't have any young couples coming for marriage at all. A man's homiletic skills might be dazzling, but they won't do a bit of good if he yells at a crying baby from the pulpit" (*Priests for the Third Millennium*, pp. 147-148).

In order to advance in these and other areas of human formation, Archbishop Dolan makes three recommendations:

- Begin each morning by dedicating that day to God and asking him for the graces necessary to attract people to him and his Church. End each day with the Examen, reviewing the times you may have hurt or offended someone and asking yourself if on that day we were bridges or obstacles for people to reach God.

- Know yourself well enough to be aware of the parts of our personalities that can attract people to Christ, and work on strengthening those traits, and to be aware of those tendencies that can drive people away, and work on eliminating those.

- Seek counsel from those you trust to be honest with you—spiritual directors, friends, counselors, bishops (Cf. *Priests for the Third Millennium*, p. 157).

"In order that his ministry may be humanly as credible and acceptable as possible, it is important that the priest should mold his human personality in such a way that it becomes a bridge and not an obstacle for others in their meeting with Jesus Christ the Redeemer of humanity. It is necessary that, following the example of Jesus who 'knew what was in humanity' (Jn. 2:25; cf. 8:3-11), the priest should be able to know the depths of the human heart, to perceive difficulties and problems, to make meeting and dialogue easy, to create trust and cooperation, to express serene and objective judgments"

—**Pope John Paul II**
*Pastores Dabo Vobis*, § 43

"All I'm saying," Archbishop Dolan writes, "is that our personality, our human nature, our character, is one of God's greatest gifts to us. As he became incarnate in the human nature of his Son, so he becomes incarnate in our human nature. Thus our humanity can become a bridge, a door, a magnet drawing people to God and his Church" (*Priests for the Third Millennium*, p. 158).

# CONVERSATION

- Who have been the agents of human formation for you and what experiences in your own life have promoted your human formation?

- *Pastores Dabo Vobis* defines four types of formation: human formation, spiritual formation, intellectual formation and pastoral formation. How have these elements of formation been helpful to you before and since ordination? Name an experience from the past six months that nourished each of these elements.

- How have your various experiences as a priest helped you become more "fully alive"?

- When you act in your ministry, in your life with family and friends, how has your formation contributed to the choices that you make?

## MISSION

*Jesus emphasized the connection between faith and action, between what we believe and what we do. In that spirit, decide on an individual or group action that flows from what you have talked about in this session. If you decide to act on your own, share your decision with the group. If you decide on a group action, determine among you whether individual members will take responsibility for various aspects of the action.*

*You are likely to benefit most from taking an action that arises from your own response to the session. However, you can consider one of the following suggestions or use these ideas to help develop one of your own:*

- The formation we have received throughout our lives, including human formation, helps us to live in the world as men who have been configured to Christ as Catholic priests.

- Write a journal entry about choices you can make that would contribute to your human formation.

- Seek out and enroll in a course or workshop that will contribute to your growth as a human being and a priest.

- Spend an evening a week reading a good novel.

- Spend time with a close friend who supports you and contributes to your growth.

- Review your health habits. If you haven't had a check-up lately, schedule one. If you're eating or drinking too much, if you're smoking, do something about it.

- Listen to Father Thomas Devery's reflection on self-care for priests in the audio book *Renewing the Priestly Heart* from RENEW International (see details at back of book).

## CLOSING PRAYER

*Facilitator:* As we conclude our time together, let us ask God to assist us in our continued growth as human beings and as his ministers.

**All: Almighty God, your Son, in his humanity, provided us with the perfect model of compassion, patience, integrity, and fidelity. As we minister to your people in his name, help us to grow continually to be more and more like him. We ask this through Christ our Lord. Amen.**

# THE PRIEST AND THE BISHOP

"My own spiritual director believes that it is precisely in obedience—not in celibacy, strangely enough—that the priest of today is most countercultural. For we live in a world that divinizes the will, holding that true happiness only comes when you have the license to do what you want, when you want, with whom and to whom you want, how you want, where you want; and that any restraint based on obedience to any higher authority is unjust, oppressive, and to be defied—since as a matter of fact, there is no 'higher authority' than my own wants, needs, and will."

—**Archbishop Timothy M. Dolan,**
*Priests for the Third Millennium*, **p. 76**

## ENVIRONMENT

*A Bible and a burning candle are placed on a small table. The Bible is open to the Scripture reading for this session. Consider decorating the table in the liturgical color for this season.*

## FOCUS OF THIS SESSION

The Church is a community made up, not only of individuals, but of smaller communities such as parishes. One of these communities is that of the bishop and his priests. This community is marked by various relationships: the sacramental relationship the bishop has with the presbyterate, the personal relationships between the bishop and the priests in the presbyterate, and the relationships that the priests have with one another.

# GATHER

## OPENING PRAYER

*Facilitator:* In *the Liturgy of the Hours,* we pray Psalm 133, which says, "How good and how pleasant it is, when brothers dwell together as one!" We know the pleasure of that from many life experiences in our families, among our relatives, in the seminary, in the parishes where we have served with other priests, in the presbyterate, or in our religious communities. We also have known the struggles that can arise among brothers. But we are called to be brothers with the bishop and in our presbyterate— brothers who labor together for the spread of the Gospel and for the building up of the Body of Christ. Let's pray as a part of the presbyterate that we might grow as brothers in the Lord.

*Facilitator:* Let us join together in offering this prayer.

**All:** **Almighty and eternal God, you sent your Son into the world to labor for the New Creation. He chose people like us to be his coworkers. Help us to work together with our bishop for the good of the Church we serve. Strengthen the bonds of friendship among us. When struggles or disrespect mark our relationships, send us your forgiving Spirit. Help us to offer all our efforts for your glory and for the welfare of your people. We ask these things of you, Father, through our Lord Jesus Christ, whose Spirit binds us together as one, forever and ever. Amen.**

### A LOOK BACK

*Facilitator:* As we gather to support one another in our renewal as priests, let's begin by talking about our present lives as men, as disciples, and as ministers.

- What have been the moments of blessing and of challenge, of joy and of frustration, in our ministry, our prayer, and our times of leisure since we last met?

- Share briefly your experience of putting into effect the action you chose to carry out after our last meeting.

## SCRIPTURE

*The facilitator invites a member of the group to read the Scripture passage.*

**1 Corinthians 3:5-9**

*Facilitator:* Let's spend a few minutes in conversation about our response to the word of God.

- What word, phrase, or image from this Scripture reading touches your heart or speaks to your life?

- How would you apply Paul's advice to your own roles as priests who are both subject to a bishop and leaders of congregations?

- How can we as priests live out Paul's declaration that only God "is anything"?

## REFLECTION

I received my current assignment six years ago. At that time I was serving as the administrator of a very small parish and as the director of a diocesan office of spiritual renewal. The manner of my change of assignment was a bit unusual. It began in the grocery store! I was there stocking up for the week. I believe I was in the canned goods aisle buying tuna fish when my cell phone rang and the caller turned out to be my archbishop. To this day, I am not sure who gave him my cell phone number. After a few pleasantries, I asked him why he was calling. The archbishop said that he wanted to change my assignment, and he mentioned the parish where he wanted me to go as pastor. The entire presbyterate knew that that parish was in great turmoil. Still standing in the canned goods aisle, I said, "Archbishop, may I ask you a question?" He said: "Yes, of course, John." "Thanks. So, are you asking me to consider this idea, and whatever I decide will be fine with you, or are you asking me to go there in obedience?" There was a pause; then he replied: "I hope you will want to go there, but I am asking you to go there in obedience." After a pause, I said, "Well, that will surely help me think about your request. But, since I'm in the middle of the grocery store, can I get back to you after I check out?"

After talking about that phone call with some friends and advisors, and after a lot of prayer, I went to see the archbishop with the intention of telling him why I thought the assignment was not a good idea, but I was also prepared to say "yes" if he persisted, because I had promised at my ordination to do so. I left his office having accepted the assignment obediently if not exactly willingly, and I am still in that parish. His request was, and continues to be, quite challenging, but it has also become a great gift.

Obedience is only one aspect of the relationship between a priest and his bishop. For some priests the foundation for our relationship with the bishop began long before we were in the seminary. It began in our homes, where we learned to relate to our parents and others in authority, whose love and care, as time passed, made us friends as well—though this is not how relationships of authority always turn out. Those of us who grew up Catholic and whose families were active in the Church also had some knowledge of, and vague connection to, the diocesan bishop through our parish and our parish priests. For some of us, the bishop in our youth may have been a figure who was larger than life. That was my experience as a child in a Catholic school, where we prayed the rosary every morning with the diocesan bishop participating over the radio. This was my first connection to a bishop. His successors were all quite different one from the other: one was quiet, warm and unassuming; another was strong and determined.

I have had a relationship with each of these men during the years that I have been a priest, and each relationship has been different—marked by positive and negative moments from my perspective and probably from theirs as well.

My experience is limited to my diocese, which is larger than some others and historically has had many diocesan priests and religious priests serving in its parishes. That has made it hard for the bishop and priests to know one another well. Still, personal contact does occur at small and large gatherings for social occasions and through opportunities for service within the presbyterate. Some of us get to know the bishop through service on the presbyteral council, others by serving as vicars in the regions of a diocese. Some of us deepen our relationship with the bishop when he comes for Confirmation and stays for dinner, or when he gathers the deanery for a luncheon meeting and time for personal conversation. Sometimes the relationship between a priest and his bishop grows in poignantly sad or joyful moments. I was very grateful to my archbishop when he came to my mother's wake and explained why he couldn't attend her funeral Mass. Conversely, some priests have

> "One priest you may not consider a friend, but one whom you as a priest should love, trust, and stay in touch with, would be your bishop. The intimate bond between a bishop and his priests is a theological necessity, which is to be a human reality as well. There is not a bishop I know who does not have the welfare of his priests as a top priority. As I have in the past, I encourage you now to remain in close contact with your bishop. An older priest I respect told me that twice each year—at the conclusion of his retreat and on the anniversary of his ordination—he would write the bishop a very personal letter, just reviewing his life and renewing to him his priestly promises. An excellent idea! Closeness with our bishop is a good insurance in protecting our priestly identity."
>
> —**Archbishop Timothy M. Dolan,**
> *Priests for the Third Millennium,* **p. 236**

thought that they became the fall guys for some decision the bishop made and they had to execute, and, in the end, felt as if they were left holding the bag. The crisis of sexual abuse of children by priests, and the added crisis of episcopal duplicity, left some priests, not only wanting, but also calling for, the resignation of their bishops. To be sure, there have been other times when the bishop felt his priests had let him down.

There is a range of experience in the relationships between priests and their bishops at both the personal and ecclesial levels. Yet, what endures through it all is the sacramental bond among us. The liturgy of the ordination of priests includes prayer for the gifts of collaboration and mutual respect between the bishop and his priests. In the consecratory prayer at the ordination of a priest, the bishop acknowledges his need for priestly collaborators and the priest promises the bishop obedience and respect. And all of this is done for the sake of spreading the Gospel to the ends of the earth.

"It is a wonderful blessing when you personally have a strong relationship, an affection, a reverence, and a deep personal loyalty to your bishop. Many of you can thank God for that. Some of you trace your vocation to the direct personal influence of your bishop. Thank God! But . . . your obedience is not to the man but to the office, and 'there will come a pharaoh who knows not Joseph.' And you will be called to respect and obey the new one as much as you did the old. Your priestly vocation, certainly your promise of obedience, is not dependent upon the man who sits in the cathedra, but to the office."

—**Archbishop Timothy M. Dolan,**
*Priests for the Third Millennium,*
**pp. 82-83**

There is one place where the connection between the priest and the bishop is clear and significant. Every day, during the Eucharistic Prayer, the priest prays for his bishop by name, and the bishop prays for all his clergy. This is the prayer that recalls and makes new the true relationship priests and bishops have with one another, with the Church, and with Christ the Lord. Let us pray that this sacrament will continue to make us and all the people entrusted to our care "one body, one spirit in Christ" (*The Roman Missal*, Eucharistic Prayer III).

# CONVERSATION

One objective of this small group of priests has been to deepen and strengthen the bonds we have been talking about today, the relationship we have with one another in the presbyterate, and our relationship with the bishop. Let us take a moment to consider and talk about these connections:

- Who have been the priests who have influenced your vocation to the priesthood? Could you share some of the stories that indicate the help they gave you?

- Recall and share occasions when your bishop helped and inspired you by word or deed.

- When have you been of help to your bishop?

- How has your understanding of the bishop's place in your life and the life of the Church grown and developed, suffered or been strengthened in your time as a priest?

## MISSION

*Jesus emphasized the connection between faith and action, between what we believe and what we do. In that spirit, decide on an individual or group action that flows from what you have talked about in this session. If you decide to act on your own, share your decision with the group. If you decide on a group action, determine among you whether individual members will take responsibility for various aspects of the action.*

*You are likely to benefit most from taking an action that arises from your own response to the session. However, if you don't sense God asking something specific of you, you can consider one of the following suggestions or use these ideas to help develop one of your own:*

- Recall a priest or bishop who has had a significant influence on your life. Choose a tangible way in which you can let him know of your gratitude.

- Each one of us may have had an encounter with a priest or bishop whom we have offended, or who has offended us. If so, choose a way to redress the hurt and reconcile.

- Commit yourself to pray each day for your bishop.

- Listen to a reflection on *Priests and Bishops: Collaborators in Ministry* by Bishop Robert N. Lynch of the Diocese of St. Petersburg, FL, in the audio book *Renewing the Priestly Heart* from RENEW International (see details at back of book).

## CLOSING PRAYER

*Facilitator:* As we conclude our time together, let's reflect on our relationship with our bishop as partners in sustaining and building up the Body of Christ.

*Pause*

*Facilitator:* Let us pray.

**All:** **Lord Jesus Christ, you provided us with the perfect model of obedience by accepting the will of your Father even to the extreme of death on a cross—a death from which you rose again to save the whole world. Help us to imitate you in our ministries by accepting with love the direction of our bishops with whom we are partners in ministering to your people. Amen.**

# THE PRIEST AND CELIBACY

"We often see celibacy in the solely negative terms of self-denial, whereas St. Paul saw it as a virtue in which the unmarried person 'can devote himself to the Lord's affairs' and worry only about pleasing the Lord (1 *Corinthians* 7:32). If celibacy is a way of devoting oneself 'to the affairs of the Lord,' then it must be a way of loving, a love that knows no rivals and provides a joyous disposition of heart for pastoral service. Defining celibacy only as giving up sex is just as unrealistic as a groom seeing marriage [only] as giving up all other women."

—**Archbishop Timothy M. Dolan,**
*Priests for the Third Millennium,* **p. 314**

## ENVIRONMENT

*A Bible and a burning candle are placed on a small table. The Bible is open to the Scripture reading for this session. Consider decorating the table in the liturgical color for this season.*

## FOCUS FOR THIS SESSION

The commitment of celibacy for a priest has two purposes. It is meant to embody and express his singular friendship with Christ, for the sake of the Church, and it is meant to express his heartfelt availability to the Church, out of love for Christ.

## GATHER

### OPENING PRAYER

*Facilitator:*  Let's spend a few moments now with our Lord Jesus and with one another in prayer.

*All:* **Lord Jesus, when you lived in Nazareth with Mary and Joseph, when you joined the community for worship at the synagogue and in the temple, when you were at prayer in the solitude of the desert or the seashore or the mountains, your Father's love and the importance of your mission compelled you. Your mission became the focus of your life, providing you with the parameters for all your decisions. Help us to follow you, to share your focus, and to root all our decisions in you and your generosity of spirit. To you, to your Father, and to the Holy Spirit, we give glory and honor, forever and ever. Amen.**

## A LOOK BACK

*Facilitator:* As we gather to support one another in our renewal as priests, let's begin by talking about our present lives as men, as disciples, and as ministers.

- What have been the moments of blessing and of challenge, of joy and of frustration, in our ministry, our prayer, and our times of leisure since we last met?

- Share briefly your experience of putting into effect the action you chose to carry out after our last meeting.

# SCRIPTURE

*The facilitator invites a member of the group to proclaim the Gospel.*

John 21:15-19

*Facilitator:* Let's spend a few minutes in conversation about our response to the word of God.

- What word, phrase, or image from this Scripture reading touches your heart or speaks to your life?

- How are you helped in your priestly life by your knowledge that Peter, after having failed Jesus several times, could sincerely make this triple affirmation of love for him?

- How does your love of Jesus, and his love for you, help you lead a celibate life?

# REFLECTION

I entered the seminary in 1972. I was eighteen years old. In some ways, it was an easy transition in my life: the seminary college was not a closed environment; we were able to take courses at other institutions, we were involved in ministerial field work, we lived a fairly well rounded life of Christian discipleship. Yet, the seminary was also very challenging because it intended to form me and the other men for the priesthood—which is a life of commitment and challenge.

It would be years before Pope John Paul II would give precise descriptions for human, spiritual, academic, and pastoral formation in his apostolic exhortation *Pastores Dabo Vobis*, yet all of these aspects of formation were happening when I entered the seminary. The faculty and the students helped me mature into an adult. This help was offered in the chapel, in spiritual direction, in the classroom, at field education sites, and in the friendship and friction among the seminarians. But all of it had one goal: personal and communal discernment regarding candidacy for the priesthood. We grew as men, our appreciation for the teachings of the Church deepened, and our spiritual lives were focused on Christ offering himself to the Father and to men, women, and children, so that "they might have life and have it more abundantly" (*John* 10:10).

In those days, many people were talking about the rule of celibacy: that it would change, that it might change, that it couldn't change. While I think many of us were intrigued by those conversations, I know our attention was focused on striving to practice a virtuous life and considering a decision for celibacy that would go hand-in-hand with being called by Christ and the Church to be priests. Members of the seminary faculty approached the reality of celibacy from the perspective of availability for the mission of the Church, and the priest's likeness to Christ, who lived his own life as a celibate. I saw celibacy as a discipline, an inner and outward personal expression of my vocation as a Catholic priest.

The challenges of celibate life are obvious in terms of sexual temptations. For some, celibacy can become only an external way of life that occasionally or regularly includes sexual encounters with women or men. This is a reality that I think most of us may have underestimated in the seminary but that has become painfully clear to us since then, at least in the experience of some of our colleagues if not in our own lives.

It would be a mistake to think that celibacy is, by its nature, impossible to live. But it also would be a mistake to think that sexual encounters priests may have with other adults exclude the possibility of forgiveness and further progress in leading celibate lives. Years ago, I heard a line in a homily that touched my mind and heart and has never left me: "If you can't always be with the Lord

"Have any of us been untouched by the tragedy of priests who have been unchaste and have ruined their lives, their ministry, have hurt innocent people, and have shamed the Church? We have seen these poor men on TV and … it seemed as if their lives were disintegrating right before our eyes. But that disintegration was long in coming. They had kept a compartment of their lives hidden, where the lights of faith and truth were never turned on. Problem is, you can never live your life for long in separate compartments. When you enter the part of your life that is dishonest or immoral, you bring your body, your soul, your reputation, and your priesthood with you. At that point, you are gambling with everything, and you risk losing everything."

—**Archbishop Timothy M. Dolan,**
*Priests for the Third Millennium*, p. 313

through virtue, you can always be with the Lord through mercy." This statement applies to any sin, including sins against celibacy. If there have been times when we have fallen short of the mark by a lack of virtue, we can still attain the goal through mercy. Both virtue and mercy are means by which we become more like Christ, and they are the experiences that lead to better friendship with him.

> "As priests, we totally, exclusively, radically, profoundly, completely—purely—belong to the Lord. He shares us with no one, and thus is able to share us with everyone. Every ounce of our strength, every urge of our affection, every drive of our libido, we freely hand over to Jesus and his Church."
>
> —Archbishop Timothy M. Dolan,
> *Priests for the Third Millennium*, p. 310

The celibate life presents other challenges. For example, the absence of a spouse and a family and the freedom of being "independent" can lead us to lives of happy bachelors—or even worse, of unhappy bachelors. We can become people who handle the deprivation celibacy entails in many ways: not just taking our days off, but seeing them as the "best part of the week"; becoming preoccupied with "stuff"; turning toward isolation, which can lead to deeper problems.

When I had been ordained for fifteen years, I had the opportunity to make the Spiritual Exercises of St. Ignatius of Loyola. During the course of those thirty days, I experienced Christ's desire to have me as his disciple, his priestly disciple. But I also experienced Christ calling me to be his friend with the same affective qualities present in any genuine, heartfelt friendship, and present in the lives of the early disciples: joy when I was in his company, companionship that focused my life, sadness and regret when I did not live up to the trust between us, and a longing to refresh and strengthen this relationship in various ways.

As all of this was being offered to me, so was a great capacity not only to be available to the Church but also to befriend the Church in appropriate and concrete ways. The experience helped me to continue to develop a professional attitude in my work as a priest that made me not only appropriate but also approachable. This singular friendship with Christ offered me many gifts, but it also offered me the desire, and hopefully a growing ability, to befriend the Church for my whole life. Every day of that retreat provided me with a palpable experience of Christ, of his love for the Father and for the disciples—and for me! It showed me, in a deeply personal way, his singularity of purpose, his firm commitment in the face of every difficulty or temptation. And through it all, I realized that I was becoming a new man through Christ by my growing, developing, affective friendship with him.

I am sure that I said many of these things earlier in my life. However, what was different after the thirty-day retreat was that I had an affective experience of Christ's befriending love that made my commitment to celibacy a way of being available, not only for the mission of the Church, but for a growing friendship with Christ. It was a friendship that would define my life, not only in external ways but internally; not just because of the ecclesial discipline of celibacy that I had promised to honor, but because of the personal friendship with Christ that I continue to experience.

## CONVERSATION

Let's take a moment to take stock of what we have heard and to consider if and how it resonates within each of us. Let's think too about how we might make some of our personal thoughts or experiences appropriately available as a means of encouragement to one another in our commitment to celibacy.

"Hence we consider that the present law of celibacy should today continue to be firmly linked to the ecclesiastical ministry. This law should support the minister in his exclusive, definitive and total choice of the unique and supreme love of Christ; it should uphold him in the entire dedication of himself to the public worship of God and to the service of the church; it should characterize his state of life both among the faithful and in the world at large."

—Pope Paul VI
*The Celibacy of the Priest,* § 14

- How has your understanding of priestly celibacy changed and matured over the years?

- What challenges have you faced in your life as a priest that have, by the gift of grace and the practice of the virtues of prudence and chastity, helped you develop a character consistent with the promises we all made at ordination to the diaconate?

- How have friendships helped you to be both loving and celibate?

### MISSION

*Jesus emphasized the connection between faith and action, between what we believe and what we do. In that spirit, decide on an individual or group action that flows from what you have talked about in this session. If you decide to act on your own, share your decision with the group. If you decide on a group action, determine among you whether individual members will take responsibility for various aspects of the action.*

*You are likely to benefit most from taking an action that arises from your own response to the session. However, if you don't sense God asking something specific of you, you can consider one of the following suggestions or use these ideas to help develop one of your own:*

- Identify a way in which we might help one another in the commitment of celibacy we made to Christ and the Church.

- Invite a friend to dinner.

- Review your life and seek help if you are habitually using pornography or are cultivating attractions to men or women.

- Listen to Father James Flavin's reflection on priestly celibacy in the audio book *Renewing the Priestly Heart* from RENEW International (see details at back of book).

## CLOSING PRAYER

*Facilitator:* In his letter, St. James reminds us to turn to the "Father of Lights, with whom there is no alteration or shadow caused by change. He willed to give us birth by the word of truth that we may be a kind of firstfruits of his creatures" (*James* 1:17). In Jesus, our Brother and Lord, we have become the sons of our Heavenly Father, and so we can pray together:

*All:* **Our Father . . . .**

# PRIESTLY CREDIBILITY AND THE SCANDALS

"Integrity is one of those traits rather tough to define but very easy to recognize. A man of integrity is a man of honesty, without guile, a genuine, authentic man, whose interior convictions are externally evident, who outwardly shows in word and deed that he is what he claims to be: a man of sincerity, truth, principle, character, and reliability, whose word can be trusted, and who inspires respect in others."

—**Archbishop Timothy M. Dolan,**
*Priests for the Third Millennium,* **p. 100**

## ENVIRONMENT

*A Bible and a burning candle are placed on a small table. The Bible is open to the Scripture reading for this session. Consider decorating the table in the liturgical color for this season.*

## FOCUS FOR THIS SESSION

Over the last fifteen years, the Church in the United States, as well as other countries, has been rocked and weakened by scandal: the sexual abuse of children by priests, the failure of the bishops to respond, embezzlement of Church funds, and clergy involved in sexual relationships with women and men. The priesthood and the Church have been deeply wounded by these scandals. Yet, Christ is with us, challenging us, and offering us his grace, to renew us and reform us, so that we might play a part in healing the broken Body of Christ.

# GATHER

## OPENING PRAYER

*Facilitator:* In our continued gathering for our renewal as priests, mindful for all that is good about the priesthood, and aware of the difficulties we face, as individuals, as a presbyterate, and as a Church, let's pause to pray.

*Pause*

**All:** **Lord our God, your Son came into a darkened world as our Light. He calmed the waters when his disciples of old were threatened in a storm at sea. He is our refuge and strength, our sure hope and our blessed destiny. Help us by his love and grace, that he might be our way, so that we might find the path to you and to a stable life in the Church. By the power of the Holy Spirit, inspire us to choose what is right and good in your sight, and to promote what is right and good in your Church, so that we might assist any and all who want to follow your Son in our company. We ask all this through Christ our Lord. Amen.**

## A LOOK BACK

*Facilitator:* As we gather to support one another in our renewal as priests, let's begin by considering and talking about our present lives as men, as disciples, and as ministers.

■ What have been the moments of blessing and of challenge, of joy and of frustration, in our ministry, our prayer, and our times of leisure since we last met?

- Share briefly your experience of putting into effect the action you chose to carry out after our last meeting.

## SCRIPTURE

*The facilitator invites a member of the group to proclaim the Gospel.*

**Matthew 17:14-20**

*Facilitator:* Let's spend a few minutes in conversation about our response to the word of God.

- What word, phrase, or image from this Scripture reading touches your heart or speaks to your life?

- How do Jesus' remarks about faith help you to believe that the broken Body of Christ can be healed from scandal and that you can play a part in the healing?

## REFLECTION

Public revelations, beginning in the 1980s, about sexual abuse of children by Catholic priests, and the failure of bishops to respond judiciously to these crimes, have eroded respect for the Church. Many people have suffered: the victims of abuse, their families, the families and parishes of accused priests, Catholics who have left the Church because of this scandal, others who have remained in the Church and have tried to maintain their faith, and priests who have been faithful to their vocations. We priests have memories of hearing about friends accused and removed from ministry; learning that members of our parish, and even our own relatives and friends, were victims.

Press reports about this issue continue to appear in the United States and abroad. Meanwhile, other things remind us of the tragedy less directly. A few weeks into 2002, for example, when each day's news included a revelation about abuse of children by priests, I was at a movie with friends. The movie had gotten great reviews. Set at the beginning of the twentieth century, it focused on the sheriff of a small Midwestern town who did his job with dedication. This character was presented as a Catholic widower with small children. At a point in the movie when the sheriff was facing a dangerous escapade, a colleague asked him if he had a plan for the children should anything happen to him. The sheriff said, "If anything happens to me, bring my children to the Reverend Jones at the Presbyterian Church. He's a good man with a good family." Then the colleague said, "Sheriff, you're a Catholic. Wouldn't your priest be able to make provisions for your children?" "No, don't bring them to Father Toolan," the sheriff said. "Bring them to Reverend Jones." The theater was filled with scornful laughter. Around that same time, some priests were saying that they were embarrassed to wear their Roman collars. I hadn't felt like that until I stopped at a toll booth on the turnpike, dressed in my Roman collar. The toll collector said: "Boy, you guys are really messed up!" I was speechless.

In addition to the revelations of clergy abuse, clergy and lay officials of the Church have been involved in other scandalous or criminal activities. Our Church has been traumatized. And the wider community, most of whom expected more from our Church, has been scandalized. Where are we today? Some of us are doing fine; some are not. Some of us are so alienated that we feel disinterested or incapable of contributing to the progress of the Church. Some have become disconnected from the priestly fraternity and from the diocese and focus all their attention on their parishes. Some think that because they are relatively young or new to the priesthood, or because cases of abuse did not affect them or their parishes directly, that the scandal and the damage it has done to the Body of Christ is irrelevant to them. Most of us are living our lives and offering our ministry for the welfare of the Church. But things have changed.

"Often have I asked what the Church, what the world, expects of priests, and I have answered my own question by responding, 'Holiness.' True enough! A very close second, and certainly related, is integrity. The Church, our people, and, yes, even the world, long for priests who are men of integrity."

—Archbishop Timothy M. Dolan, *Priests for the Third Millennium*, p. 100

As the crisis unfolded, priests, parish council members, religious education directors, pastoral associates, and Voice of the Faithful groups were looking for spiritual renewal opportunities. At that time, I was serving in our diocesan Office of Spiritual Development. Our staff received inquiries from individuals and groups who wanted assistance. As we grappled with the crisis and with ways to help those who sought our services, two mysteries of our faith proved helpful to us and to the groups we served. The first mystery—the Father's plan in sending his Son into the world—rested on a passage from the Second Letter of St. Paul to the Corinthians that we hear on Ash Wednesday:

"For our sake he made him to be sin, so that we might become the righteousness of God in him" (2 *Corinthians* 5:21).

None of us, nor the groups with whom we worked, doubted the sinfulness of the behavior of some priests and the grave offense of covering up the abuse. But, all of us who believe in Christ understand that he does not stay safely distant from our sins, working our redemption from afar. Rather, as St. Paul understood from his own experience, Christ takes the worst in us to himself so that he can offer us in return the gifts of his wisdom, love, and grace. This mystery resonated with us, as a staff, and with many other members of the Church. The other mystery of faith that proved helpful in our ministry to all kinds of people in the throes of the crisis was found in the Risen Christ himself. The Risen Christ appeared on Easter day with his wounds visible to the disciples. The Risen Christ is wounded. His wounds enabled the first disciples to know it was really him (cf. *John* 20:20). It was only when they saw his wounds that they could rejoice and receive the new life that he offered. Christ's wounds verify his suffering and offer, in an intimate and tangible way, a real share in his new life. His wounds are no longer death-dealing, but life-giving to those who have been traumatized. In the First Letter of St. Peter, we read more about these life-giving wounds. St. Peter repeatedly benefited from the mercy of the Risen Lord: in the upper room, on Easter, and on the shores of the Sea of Tiberias where Jesus asked, "Simon, do you love me?" "Yes, Lord, you know that I love you." The Lord's response entailed responsibility: "Feed my sheep!" Peter, wounded by his failure at a time that called for heroic action, was being healed by the wounded Risen Lord (*John* 21:15-17). In this way, as in so many others, Peter is not only the leader of the Eleven, but the symbol of the Church's weakness and sin, and the manifestation of what the Lord's grace can accomplish in us. This allowed Peter to proclaim, in his first letter, what the Risen Christ intends to do for all of us—to heal us by his wounds (cf. *1 Peter* 2:24). There is a double mystery: the Church, as his body in the world, is always wounded. At the same time, the healing that the Church always needs comes from her wounded Lord.

> "Now, a second help to obtaining and sustaining integrity is the ability to hear the truth about yourself. For, if it is true that "it's desperately difficult to be honest with yourself," we will need to cherish people of integrity who will tell us the truth about ourselves, even when it stings. I mentioned that people expect their priests to preach the truth; well, a priest of integrity should likewise be willing to hear the truth!"
>
> —**Archbishop Timothy M. Dolan**, *Priests for the Third Millennium*, p. 107

Sins committed by some priests and bishops have not changed our vocation. These events have not abrogated our call to respond to the challenge Jesus made to Peter: "Feed my sheep." If anything, the crisis has made our response more urgent. Dioceses have taken steps to assure the safety of children who are under the supervision or care of priests and other church personnel, but we are called to go beyond those institutional policies and be bridges of healing and reconciliation in the Church and in the world.

Within our own congregations, we priests can emphasize in our homilies, in our interactions with catechists, and in our private conversations, the fundamental Christian belief that life came from death in the resurrection of Jesus and that renewal can come from this scandal. We can remind our parishioners that the same belief applies to our own lives—that we all sin but we all can rise again through the grace of penance and the Eucharist, sacraments that are not diminished by the human failings of the Church. We can help our parishioners—some of whom may feel powerless in the trauma suffered by their church—that they are equal members of the Body of Christ and they have a share in the mission of evangelizing the world by living the Gospel every day.

By being present and attentive in these ways, we can play our role in healing the Church and restoring its place in the community as a trusted agent of charity and social justice.

## CONVERSATION

We have seen much of the Lord's dying and rising in these years marked by scandal, criminal behavior, and shame; and by efforts to protect children and other vulnerable people, and restore confidence and trust, so that we can continue our mission in the world.

- As you recall the onslaught of revelations about clergy sexual abuse, and other scandalous activity, what helped you live day to day?

- As you consider life in the Church in the last 10 to 15 years, and the various efforts that have been made to make the Church safe for the vulnerable, what efforts have been successful, and what still needs to be done?

- As a priest, how would you assess the toll that the scandals have taken on you and the Church? Where do you see evidence of new life and progress happening in Christ's body, the Church? What are some tangible ways you can contribute to the ongoing reform and growth of the Church and the priesthood?

# MISSION

*Jesus emphasized the connection between faith and action, between what we believe and what we do. In that spirit, decide on an individual or group action that flows from what you have talked about in this session. If you decide to act on your own, share your decision with the group. If you decide on a group action, determine among you whether individual members will take responsibility for various aspects of the action.*

*You are likely to benefit most from taking an action that arises from your own response to the session. However, if you don't sense God asking something specific of you, you can consider one of the following suggestions or use these ideas to help develop one of your own:*

"I know some will brand me hopelessly naïve because of this observation, but I detect in the Church today a grassroots movement calling us all to a profound appreciation of the Lord's mercy. In the midst of the crisis, crime, immorality, violence, hatred, injustice, and evil of the 'civilization of hate,' or 'the culture of death,' God's people are again recognizing the overwhelming power of his mercy."

—**Archbishop Timothy M. Dolan**, *Priests for the Third Millennium*, **pp. 240-241**

- Phone or write to someone whom you feel has suffered in some way from the scandal in the Church, and offer your support or encouragement.

- Encourage parishioners who feel betrayed or disillusioned to discuss their concerns with you.

- Hold an evening of eucharistic adoration to pray for healing in the church.

- Be as visible as possible in your parish and in your community. Avoid being defensive about what has happened in the church and instead seek opportunities for evangelization.

■ Reinforce the perception of lay men and women that they are essential members of the Body of Christ and share fully in the opportunity to help it learn from the scandal, recover from its wounds, and move on in its evangelistic mission.

■ Commit yourself to praying to the Holy Spirit to guide the laity and clergy in healing the Body of Christ.

■ Listen to Monsignor Robert Silva's reflection on recovering from the sexual-abuse scandal in the Church in the audio book *Renewing the Priestly Heart* from RENEW International (see details at back of book).

# CLOSING PRAYER

*Facilitator:* St. Paul tells us that where sin increases grace overflows even more (*Romans* 5:20). Let us pray for God's grace to touch the lives of everyone affected by sin in the Church:

*All:* **Almighty God, because of the sin of Adam, you sent your only Son to be our Redeemer. His body was broken on the cross, but he overcame death and won for us the promise of eternal life. May his word and example lead those who have sinned in any way to a conversion of heart. May our gratitude for his unselfish love inspire us to commit ourselves again to our vocation and devote our energy and talents to healing the Body of Christ, your Church.**

**We ask this through the same Jesus Christ, your Son, our Lord, who lives and reigns with you and the Holy Spirit, one God, for ever and ever. Amen.**

# THE PRIEST AND THE SACRAMENTS

"While a recognition of this truth, that Jesus comes to us in mystery in the Holy Eucharist, is essential to all in the Church, the priest especially must exude an awe about this mysterious presence, a profound faith in its reality, a constant hunger for this heavenly food, a ready desire to savor his presence in this sacrament, and an exuberance about telling others of this sacred gift."

—**Archbishop Timothy M. Dolan,**
*Priests for the Third Millennium*, **p. 213**

## ENVIRONMENT

*A Bible and a burning candle are placed on a small table. The Bible is open to the Scripture reading for this session. Consider decorating the table in the liturgical color for this season.*

## FOCUS FOR THIS SESSION

In addition to the ministry of proclaiming the Gospel, we priests offer the sacraments in the community of faith. Yet, like the word we preach, the sacraments we celebrate aren't gifts only for the people, but moments of grace for us as well. All of these experiences renew and deepen our personal configuration to Christ and our capacity to bring Christ to others.

## GATHER

### OPENING PRAYER

*Facilitator:* As we prepare to continue our reflection on our common vocation to the priesthood of Christ, let us take a moment for quiet prayer.

*Pause*

**All:** **Almighty God, Father of our Lord Jesus Christ and our Father too, open our hearts to hear the voice of your Son and to feel the effects of his love and grace in our lives. Help us to see and hear and feel him as we participate with him in the celebration of the sacraments by which all of his people are reborn and renewed. We ask these things in the name of your Son, who lives and reigns forever and ever. Amen.**

## A LOOK BACK

*Facilitator:* As we gather to support one another in our renewal as priests, let's begin by considering talking about our present lives as men, as disciples, and as ministers.

- What have been the moments of blessing and of challenge, of joy and of frustration, in our ministry, our prayer, and our times of leisure?

- Share briefly your experience of putting into effect the action you chose to carry out after our last meeting.

# SCRIPTURE

*The facilitator invites a member of the group to proclaim the Gospel.*

Mark 6:6b-13, 30-44

*Facilitator:* Let's spend a few minutes in conversation about our response to the word of God.

- What word, phrase, or image from this Scripture reading touches your heart or speaks to your life?

- How do you balance your zeal for your ministry with the desire to say yes to every request for help?

# REFLECTION

I got a call one Sunday evening from a priest friend. When I answered the phone he launched right in: "It's been a crazy day! I had three Masses this morning and one last night. I had a wedding after Mass last night and baptisms this afternoon. I just got back home when the hospital called, and there were a few people who needed to be anointed. Then, after I had a sandwich, I went over to the parish center to meet with the confirmation candidates. It was a crazy day, but it was a good one—I think!"

Everyone has days like that, crammed with all kinds of activities. It is no less true for priests who every day encounter people with different spiritual and emotional needs. The experience can make us weary. A fourteen-hour day takes a physical toll, and the work itself can leave us feeling burdened. I think the disciples, and Jesus himself, at times shared these feelings. I think this is what underlies a portion of the sixth chapter of St. Mark's Gospel. Jesus had sent the disciples on a mission almost empty handed: no food, no money, no change of clothes. They were to take only a walking stick and a second pair of sandals. I presume these were to help the tough keep going when the going was tough.

When the disciples returned, Jesus invited them to get into the boat and rest for a while. Whenever I read this passage, I imagine that the disciples thought Jesus was taking them on the first century's version of a Club Med vacation. However, it was only a ferry ride to the other side of the lake, where the crowds, and the work, were waiting.

I am sure that the disciples groaned. Jesus, however, was passionate about the people and their needs. St. Mark tells us that Jesus taught them "many things." Jesus was also aware that the crowd was hungry, not only for the Word, but for food. And so, the bread and the fish that the disciples had brought for themselves became more than enough for the vast crowd because of Jesus' love and power. The disciples labored to distribute the bread and the fish to the crowd, and to gather up the leftovers, but they too must have been nourished and refreshed.

I think something similar happens in our lives. The way my friend felt on that Sunday night is not an uncommon experience for us. But it seems to me that more happened in his day than work, and more resulted from his day than exhaustion. He described the day to me in some detail. He talked about the families who came to Mass, and he said he imagined, as they were coming to Holy Communion together, how this encounter with Christ would strengthen and support their family life. He told me about the delight he took, not only in the joy and hope on the faces of the parents whose children he baptized, but in their heartfelt responses to the ritual questions. Then he spoke about a man who had received the sacrament of the sick in the hospital. The man, who had Parkinson's disease, had been admitted for a heart procedure. This man was very worried about the procedure, and his anxiety had exacerbated his tremors. After they prayed together, and after the man was anointed, my friend noticed that the tremors seemed less pronounced. He said to me: "Don't get me wrong. I am

> "I submit that it is an essential part of spiritual stewardship for us to ask ourselves these questions ceaselessly as we examine our consciences about faith....
>
> "Do we believe God is alive and powerful in the prayers he answers and in the Church born from the opened side of his Son, that he continues to act in his seven sacraments, which really work and accomplish what they signify; that by baptism we became children of God and temples of the Holy Spirit; that in Eucharist we really and truly receive our Lord, body, blood, soul, and divinity; that in the sacrament of penance our sins are really forgiven?"
>
> —Archbishop Timothy M. Dolan,
> *Priests for the Third Millennium,*
> pp. 21-22

not saying he was cured, but, obviously, the Lord lessened his fear." I know my friend well enough to say that he had both an exhausting and a refreshing day. It was a day that was both jammed with work and charged with grace.

The tasks that filled my friend's day were occasions for grace not only for those whom he served but also for him. It often works that way for me, too; I suspect it works that way for all of us. All of the sacraments are powerful experiences for the immediate participants, but also for the gathered community—including the priest. As we remember the death and resurrection of Christ, the Risen Lord touches the entire assembly to promote his saving work in each and all of us. As priests, we are not only at the service of this transformation; we are, at the same time, being offered the saving work of Christ the Priest. We are not only the members of the Church who offer these gifts of Christ to his people; we ourselves are constantly renewed by these sacred signs. On the day we were ordained, when the bishop handed us the paten with bread and the chalice with wine, he said to each of us, "Accept from the holy people of God the gifts to be offered to him. Know what you are doing, and imitate the mystery you celebrate; model your life on the mystery of the Lord's cross" (*The Rites of the Catholic Church*, Volume II, Ordination of a Priest, p. 68). This charge can seem daunting, and it would be if its accomplishment depended solely on our deliberate choices. However, we go to the altar daily, we visit the hospital regularly, we listen to confessions routinely. Sundays often include baptisms or weddings. We are not only facilitating the encounter our people have

"At the seminary, we prepare men for a life where the most important service they will perform for their people is to—especially on the Lord's day—celebrate the Eucharist for them, sometimes even two or three times a day; where the most effective service you can perform for the sick is to anoint them; where you can do nothing better for a family than to baptize their babies; where you can do for the burdened soul what no one else can, namely forgive their sins in the sacrament of penance; where you can be of no greater aid to the dying than by bringing Viaticum. Don't aspire to the parish priesthood unless you believe this!"

—Archbishop Timothy M. Dolan, *Priests for the Third Millennium*, p. 272

with Christ in the sacraments; we are encountering Christ ourselves.

Archbishop Dolan points out that the wonderful increase in lay ministry has led some to the erroneous conclusion that priests are being "reduced" to sacramental ministry. While priests are busy with many other things, the archbishop writes, "there is nothing he can do to help his people more than to give them the sacraments … I always thought the joy of our vocation was in being 'elevated' to being sacramental ministers! Granted, there is legitimate cause for caution lest a parish priest become robotic, mechanistic, a mere functionary in his celebration of the sacraments. But, if we believe in the utter power of the sacraments, if we are convinced that there is nothing better we can do to assist our people than to bring them the sacraments, that will not happen. We are most a pastor when we are administering the sacraments" (*Priests for the Third Millennium*, p. 271).

St. Ignatius of Loyola challenged the Jesuits that if their ministerial obligations prevented them from completing their daily prayer and meditation, they should never omit the Examen. Ignatius understood that the Examen was not just an examination of conscience for the purpose of celebrating the sacrament of penance, but it was also a contemplative exploration of our daily experience as the followers of Christ. This kind of prayer allows us to see where the Lord is working on our behalf, with a view to strengthening our faith and enabling us to respond to his persistent call to serve and to be served by him. The Examen is one element of the reflective life to which we are called as Christians and as priests. I have found the practice of Examen helpful. There is a real benefit to this prayerful review of the day, looking simply to see how the work of ministry not only provided others with experiences of Christ but offered us the same. On the day of my first Mass, the Gospel appointed for that Sunday was *Matthew* 9:36-10:8, the last line of which, in a current translation, says: "Without cost you have received; without cost you are to give" (*Matthew* 10:8). When I was ordained thirty years ago, an earlier translation of the Gospel said: "The gift you have received, give as a gift." I think we do this, as priests, all the time. But I think it works in reverse for us as well—the gift we give, we receive as a gift. The gifts we give to people with whom we celebrate the sacraments become Christ's gift of himself to us, his priests.

## CONVERSATION

*Facilitator:* Christ is constantly touching our hearts and minds with grace. Today, we have considered our sacramental ministry not just as an aspect of our ministry to the members of the Church, but also as an experience of Christ's care for us as his priestly disciples. We are called to assist one another as brother priests. Let's take a moment to consider what we have shared today so that we might offer one another something of ourselves and our faith.

- Having reflected on the priesthood of Christ and his sacramental presence, not only to the men, women and children in the liturgical assembly, but to you as well, how do you experience the palpable presence of Christ at the liturgy or in the sacraments?

- Are these manifestations of grace part of your regular experience, do they come only at turning points in your life, or do they come rarely if at all?

- When you have felt these offers of grace, manifestations of Christ's presence, where do they tend to lead you?

## MISSION

*Jesus emphasized the connection between faith and action, between what we believe and what we do. In that spirit, decide on an individual or group action that flows from what you have talked about in this session. If you decide to act on your own, share your decision with the group. If you decide on a group action, determine among you whether individual members will take responsibility for various aspects of the action.*

*You are likely to benefit most from taking an action that arises from your own response to the session. However, if you don't sense God asking something specific of you, you can consider one of the following suggestions or use these ideas to help develop one of your own:*

- Begin each celebration of a sacrament with a brief, spontaneous prayer in which you thank God for calling you to this unique ministry.

- Ask someone you trust to closely observe you as you celebrate the Eucharist or baptism and offer you input on what is most effective about your approach and what could be improved.

- Review the Sunday readings for the next few months and plan a series of homilies in which you use the Gospel to refresh your congregation's awareness of the grace God offers in the sacraments of baptism, confirmation, penance, Eucharist, matrimony, and anointing of the sick. Share these with a priest friend.

## CLOSING PRAYER

*Facilitator:* When we were ordained, our hands were anointed so that we might lead people to love God through the example of our lives and through the celebration of the sacraments. Let's pray together that God might help us continue to grow in enthusiasm and effectiveness in our vocation.

*All:* **Almighty God, you have called us to be the visible presence to your people of the one** high priest, our Lord Jesus Christ. You have given us the privilege of acting in his place, through sacred signs, to make your divine life accessible to your people. Strengthen our faith in the sacraments and renew our awareness of the vital service we perform for your people. We ask this through your Son, our Lord Jesus Christ, who lives and reigns with you in the unity of the Holy Spirit, one God, forever and ever. Amen.

# THE PRIEST AND THE HOMILY

"In your prayer, in your study, in your friendships, in your daily experiences, in your travel, in your reading, in art, drama, literature, movies, history . . . in all things, glean lessons, examples, and images that can be used in the pulpit. We are so in love with Jesus, so committed to his truth, that we are forever looking for ways to preach him and his truth with enthusiasm and cogency."

—**Archbishop Timothy M. Dolan,**
*Priests for the Third Millennium*, **p. 305**

## ENVIRONMENT

*A Bible and a burning candle are placed on a small table. The Bible is open to the Scripture reading for this session. Consider decorating the table in the liturgical color for this season.*

## FOCUS FOR THIS SESSION

Preaching is a primary ministry of the priest. Preaching is not only a commission that is given but an art that is developed. Life experience, prayer, and study help hone the art and fulfill the commission to preach.

## GATHER

### OPENING PRAYER

*Facilitator:*   We are disciples gathered in the Lord, who know the sound of his voice, who have heard his call and have chosen to follow him. Let's take a moment to speak to him from our hearts.

*Pause*

*All:* **Lord, you have called us to be both hearers and heralds of your word. Open our minds and hearts to ponder the word, so that it may touch and change our lives. Give us the gifts we need to announce the word with loving conviction to those entrusted to our care. Make us doers of the word, not only hearers, living gospels, not only preachers, for the wellbeing of the people you have called to be your disciples in the world. To you, to your Father, and to the Holy Spirit, we give glory and honor, now and always and forever and ever. Amen.**

## A LOOK BACK

*Facilitator:* As we gather to support one another in our renewal as priests, let's begin by considering and talking about our present lives as men, as disciples, and as ministers.

- What have been the moments of blessing and of challenge, of joy and of frustration, in our ministry, our prayer, and our times of leisure since we last met?

- Share briefly your experience of putting into effect the action you chose to carry out after our last meeting.

# SCRIPTURE

*The facilitator invites a member of the group to read the Scripture passage:*

**2 Corinthians 12:3-10**

*Facilitator:* Let's spend a few minutes in conversation about our response to the word of God.

- What word, phrase, or image from this Scripture reading touches your heart or speaks to your life?

- How do you think Paul's relationship with the Christians in Corinth was helped by his willingness to share his personal experience so freely?

- Do you ever use experiences from your own life of faith or prayer in your homilies? If so, is it comfortable for you? If not, does this example from Paul give you some incentive to do so?

## REFLECTION

While Archbishop Dolan was rector of the North American College in Rome, a frieze in the college chapel, depicting the sacraments of the church, got his attention. While there are seven sacraments, he writes in *Priests for the Third Millennium,* "there are eight scenes on the frieze! What's the eighth one? In the lower corner to the left is a scene of a priest preaching! It is almost as if the artist was telling future priests that there was an eighth sacrament, preaching!" (*Priests for the Third Millennium,* p. 295) The Second Vatican Council, in fact, declared that the "priests . . . have the primary duty of proclaiming the Gospel of God to all" (*The Decree on the Ministry and Life of Priests* § 4). While a priest may carry out that duty directly and indirectly in a variety of ways—including by the example of his life—he carries it out most explicitly when he preaches.

I love to preach, and, while I never doubted the importance of preaching, especially at the Sunday Eucharist, I have not always loved it. As a young deacon and priest, I found it difficult. When I was a deacon, preaching mostly in the seminary to my peers and professors felt quite daunting. In some ways, I figured that preaching could only get easier after ordination to the priesthood, when I would be preaching in a parish. I was wrong. I still found preaching difficult in my first assignment as a priest. As I look back on it now, I see that one of the problems was an incomplete appreciation of preaching. Don't get me wrong: I think the homiletics course in the seminary was quite good. The problem wasn't about the techniques, the theory, or the practice. It was about my self-awareness. I thought preaching was just one element in the priest's job description. That was the problem. Over the years, I've come to realize that preaching is an essential part of my vocation and spirituality as a priest.

The spiritual director who led my ordination retreat encouraged us to develop a Sunday night habit of reading the Scripture passages, especially the Gospel, for the next Sunday, as a lens for the week. As a young priest, I tried to do that, and it has become a habit. It allows me to prayerfully consider the Gospel passage throughout the week, to see the connections between the Scripture and life. It allows me to preach in a way that both emerges from my prayer and links the Gospel and life together. It has moved me from thinking of the homily as teaching to thinking of the homily as preaching. In his preaching, Jesus always used aspects of ordinary life to disclose how faith works in the lives of real people. The Second Vatican Council confirmed, with respect to preaching, that "the word of God ought not to be explained in a general and abstract way, but rather by applying the lasting truth of the Gospel to the particular circumstances of life" (*The Decree on the Ministry and Life of Priests* § 4). As Archbishop

> "It's very convenient today to avoid preaching the cross, because therapeutic, feel-good, affirming, self-help, New Age, self-fulfillment themes are the new orthodoxy ...
>
> "This is the culture that needs to be confronted with the cross. To preach pro-life in a suburban parish today is to preach the cross! To preach chastity on a college campus is to preach the cross! To preach on the danger of riches and the demands of social justice to an affluent congregation is to preach the cross! To preach the preference for dialogue, patience, and diplomacy over military action at an army base is to preach the cross! But preach Christ crucified we must!"
>
> —**Archbishop Timothy M. Dolan,** *Priests for the Third Millennium*, **p. 301**

Dolan observed in the passage that began this session, we can achieve this goal by gathering images, examples, and lessons for our homilies by being alert to what we see and hear every day in our work, our travels, our recreation, our reading, our conversations.

I have also learned that these links to life are assisted by study, that is, by using resources that expand our personal understanding of the sacred texts. As God's Word, the Biblical texts are filled with meaning and nuances that surpass our first impressions, and even a lifetime of impressions. Part of the benefit of our membership in the Church is the rich body of reflections from brothers and sisters in the faith, living and dead, ancient and modern. There are many ways of accessing this wisdom today, but one way is to develop a small preaching library (both in print and online) of solid scriptural commentaries to enrich our understanding of the texts as the word of the Lord. This is part and parcel of the responsibility bestowed on us as men whose vocation is to preach. This aspect of our vocation both enriches our own spiritual lives by the wisdom of others and assists us in deepening our personal understanding, appreciation, and exposition of the God's word.

"Sincerity ... requires that we must be ourselves in the pulpit. Gimmicks, or imposed recipes for model sermons, or trying to be someone we are not, or depending on homily notes, backfire. Margaret Melady did her doctoral dissertation on an analysis of the communication style of John Paul II. She found that for all his talks—audiences, public events, addresses to heads of state, visits around the world—for all his talks but one, he depended on the help of his advisers. The one style of communication he personally wrote all alone was a homily. That should not surprise us, because how else could a sermon be sincere?"

—Archbishop Timothy M. Dolan,
*Priests for the Third Millennium,*
pp. 303-304

In his landmark document *On Evangelization in the Modern World,* Pope Paul VI wrote, "Modern man listens more willingly to witnesses than to teachers, and if he does listen to teachers, it is because they are witnesses" (*Evangelii Nuntiandi,* § 41, Jan. 8, 1975). Our vocation to be preachers requires not only our solid thought but also the witness of our lives. In this regard, I mean not only our efforts in leading a life of authenticity, but in sharing something of ourselves with the members of the Church in our preaching. There is an old adage to this effect: "If you want people to weep, you need to use your own handkerchief." This adage isn't promoting theatrics; rather, it is encouraging personal witness. For our purposes, it suggests that the homilist must ground his reflections in the reality of his own life of conversion. Our lives, like the lives of the people entrusted to our care, are not lives of steady progress in the Christian life; rather, they are lives marked by growth, backsliding, and renewed progress, and all with the Lord's constant help. If preaching aims at personal and communal conversion, it suggests to me that we need to offer, in appropriate ways, our own experience as witnesses to the dynamic nature of conversion. It is one way that we can indicate that the perfection offered by the Christian life is attained only by means of progress that comes through fits and starts but is constantly assisted by grace.

Many priests have found the prayerful approach of *Lectio* Divina to be an invaluable aid in their preaching—the unhurried reading (*lectio*) of a Scripture passage in which we are aware of God's presence in his word listen for the words or verse that resonate with us personally here and now; the reflection (*meditatio*), in which we reflect on the verses, re-read and repeat them, and ask ourselves what God is saying, what he is calling us to; the prayerful dialogue with God (*oratio*), in which we accept this more intimate understanding of his will, and the silent contemplation of his presence, his message, and his will. Opening ourselves to what God is saying to us beyond the literal meaning of Scriptures can help us to open the Scriptures to the assembly of God's people so that they can see its relevance to their own lives. (Father Ed Griswold, who teaches homiletics at St. Mary's Seminary and University in Baltimore, Md., discusses

> "Never, ever, subject your people to what you have had to go through! Make a list—I'm serious—make a list of the bad pulpit habits that drive you wild. Again, I'm talking natural, human flaws: the mumbling, the slavery to a text, the voice you can barely hear, the auctioneer pace, the homilies where we check not our watch but our calendar, all the things that have often made homilies unbearable—and, for God's sake, don't do them!
>
> —Archbishop Timothy M. Dolan, *Priests for the Third Millennium*, p. 297

"Some years ago a survey was taken among a group of parishioners. They were asked what they hoped to experience during a sermon. When the results were in, the answer was clear. What the majority wanted was simply to hear a person of faith speaking. Ultimately, that's what preaching is all about, not lofty theological speculation, not painstaking biblical exegesis, not oratorical flamboyance. The preacher is a person speaking to people about faith and life."

*—Fulfilled in Your Hearing – the Homily in the Sunday Assembly, § 39*

*Lectio Divina* and homily preparation on pages 106-110 of this book.)

Finally, most Catholics hear the homily during the celebration of the Eucharist. The connection between the homily and the sacrament is crucial. When I preach at Mass, I try, whenever possible, to reveal an aspect of the Holy Eucharist suggested by the Liturgy of the Word. All of the sacraments are the objects of people's faith, and that faith is nourished by the word of God which we, as priest-celebrants, have the primary obligation to proclaim. "This is especially true of the Liturgy of the Word in the celebration of Mass, in which the proclaiming of the death and resurrection of Christ is inseparably joined to the response of the people who hear, and to the very offering whereby Christ ratified the New Testament with his blood"(*Decree on the Ministry and Life of Priests*, § 4).

## CONVERSATION

As we continue to consider our vocation as preachers, let's reflect on these questions and talk about our responses:

- As you consider your life as a priest, and all the responsibilities you have, what place does the Sunday homily hold on list of work priorities?

- How has your understanding of preaching evolved over the years?

- How do you prepare your homily for Sunday? What challenges do you face? What are some of the preaching resources that you find most helpful?

# MISSION

*Jesus emphasized the connection between faith and action, between what we believe and what we do. In that spirit, decide on an individual or group action that flows from what you have talked about in this session. If you decide to act on your own, share your decision with the group. If you decide on a group action, determine among you whether individual members will take responsibility for various aspects of the action.*

*You are likely to benefit most from taking an action that arises from your own response to the session. However, if you don't sense God asking something specific of you, you can consider one of the following suggestions or use these ideas to help develop one of your own:*

- Choose a Sunday, and solicit feedback on your preaching from your community or from your staff. Provide a form or a card for responses, and ask specific questions: What did I say to you in the homily? What suggestion do you have about the content of the homily? What suggestion do you have about my preaching style?

- This Sunday and hereafter, read and pray over the readings for the following Sunday. Each day, re-read the Scriptures and look for connections with your life. Ask others in the parish what these Scriptures say to them to help you see God at work in people's lives.

- Read Father Edward J. Griswold's discussion of *Lectio Divina* and homiletics preparation on pages 106–110, and listen

"A homily is not a talk given on the occasion of a liturgical celebration. It is "a part of the liturgy itself." In the Eucharistic celebration the homily points to the presence of God in people's lives and then leads a congregation into the Eucharist, providing, as it were, the motive for celebrating the Eucharist in this time and place" (Cf. *Lectionary for Mass.* English translation of the Second Editio-Typica (1981) #24 prepared by International Commission on English in the Liturgy).

*—Fulfilled in Your Hearing – the Homily in the Sunday Assembly, § 60*

to his presentation in the audio book that accompanies *Renewing the Priestly Heart* (see details at back of book).

# CLOSING PRAYER

*All:*  **Almighty Father**
**In his ministry your Son helped your people see how the commandment to love God and neighbor applied to the realities of daily life. Help us to follow his example by being alert to what we see and hear every day, in our work, in our study, and in our leisure, and use our experience to call your people to both profess their faith and lead faith-filled lives.**

**We ask this through your Son, Jesus Christ, who lives and reigns with you and the Holy Spirit, one God, forever and ever. Amen.**

# THE PRIEST AND LIFELONG LEARNING

"The spiritual life is not a tidy, isolated compartment of our existence! No, as the Holy Father says, 'Spiritual formation is the core which unifies and gives life to our entire being.' Thus, every element of our lives is part of the spiritual arena, and growth in holiness will entail wholehearted immersion in a spiritual regimen. ...

"Academic rigor plays a part as well, through consistent study and research, ongoing reading, theological refinement, and the cultivation of good reading habits."

—**Archbishop Timothy M. Dolan,**
*Priests for the Third Millennium,* **p. 19**

## ENVIRONMENT

*A Bible and a burning candle are placed on a small table. The Bible is open to the Scripture reading for this session. Consider decorating the table in the liturgical color for this season.*

## FOCUS OF THIS SESSION

Discipleship is never ending for members of the Church, especially for leaders. This awareness has implications for various aspects of our lives. All of adult learning can assist us in becoming the men and the priests that the Lord called us to be in the diverse community of his Church

## GATHER

### OPENING PRAYER

*Facilitator:* As we continue our time together, let's take a few moments for quiet prayer, so that we can be available to the Lord, who is always present to us.

*All:* **Lord, in the writings of St. Luke, we are consoled, that "we live and move and have our being" in you (*Acts* 17:28). Help us to continue to abide in you, as we confidently believe you will abide in us. May we continue to grow in you, with all the people we serve, so that we may come to the fullness of life and love. Breathe the Holy Spirit upon us in our time together today, so that we might grow in our appreciation of you and your word. Continue to empower us to announce the word in ways that renew our communities of faith. Keep us all on the way that leads to you. May all glory and honor be given to you, to your Father, and to the Holy Spirit, forever and ever. Amen.**

## SONG SUGGESTION

## A LOOK BACK

*Facilitator:* As we gather to support one another in our renewal as priests, let's begin by considering our present lives as men, as disciples, and as ministers.

■ What have been the moments of blessing and of challenge, of joy and of frustration, in our ministry, our prayer, and our times of leisure since we last met?

■ Share briefly your experience of putting into effect the action you chose to carry out after our last meeting.

# SCRIPTURE

*The facilitator invites a member of the group to proclaim the Gospel.*

**Luke 13:6-9**

- What word, phrase, or image from this Scripture reading touches your heart or speaks to your life?

- What concrete steps have you taken in the past five years to continue your formation as a man and as a priest?

# REFLECTION

One of the realities of being a pastor has been working with the finance council. And for me, one of the challenges involved in working with the finance council has been learning to understand a balance sheet. I can balance my own checkbook—most days. However, I would never risk preparing my own taxes. A few good things have happened since I learned to read a balance sheet. First, I follow the discussions at the finance council better than I did in the past. Second, I have developed greater respect for the talent the members of the finance council bring to the Church. And last, but by no means least, I realize that I am still able to learn new things, useful things, to benefit my ministry in the Church, and not just for preaching or pastoral care. Now I am not only a cheerleader for the way the finance council and business manager help the parish; I am a real colleague in the work—though, I still wouldn't risk doing my own taxes. This learning has helped me see the benefits of a broad approach to lifelong learning.

"You hear more and more from spiritual directors, therapists, and self-help experts that a careful, planned, regular daily regimen, balancing prayer, study, work, recreation, exercise, time for friends, eating, sleep—is good insurance for a healthy, happy life. No matter where we are or what we're doing, no matter if here or on vacation, certain things are constant ... But there are others, from proper sleep and exercise, time for friends and reading ...."

—**Archbishop Timothy M. Dolan,** *Priests for the Third Millennium*, p. 73

None of this should be foreign to us. Pope John Paul II taught us clearly that formation is ongoing, and not only in theology, spirituality, homiletics and pastoral care. Lifelong learning should be second nature to us because we have been baptized and ordained to be lifelong learners, that is, priest-disciples. Our teacher and master, Jesus our Lord, was a lifelong learner. He learned to pray with Mary and Joseph. He learned the Scriptures with the teachers in the synagogue. Jesus certainly learned to become a carpenter by watching Joseph and then by being his apprentice. These simple experiences nurtured a curiosity in Jesus, a desire to learn. This led him to learn all kinds of things. He knew something about caring for fruitless fig trees. He was intrigued by the training, dedication, and generosity of pearl merchants. His friends and disciples clearly influenced him regarding the proper times and ways to fish—and he was able to provide counterintuitive wisdom even to experienced fishermen.

> "Of greatest value in my priesthood has been participating with lay people in small faith-sharing groups. It is in this setting that I have best come to know the realities of parishioners' lives, their hopes, the difficulties they face, and their spiritual aspirations. At the same time, without their realizing it, they have helped and challenged me to know what they look for in me as a priest, how to preach in a more meaningful way, and how to realistically best serve them in their daily lives. The greatest formation in my priesthood has come from being in faith-sharing community with parishioners."
>
> —**Msgr. Tom Kleissler**
> **Co-Founder, RENEW International**

We come to our vocation not only as students of religion but also as men who were exposed to varied experiences as we made our way through life: early on, we noticed how human relationships work, for woe and for weal. As we grew up in the country, in small towns, or in cities; as we found careers and left them with an education that the seminary never provided, we were being formed. Some of us have peer-like conversations with pianists, college professors, hockey players, or store managers. We are men with a range of talents, interests, professional backgrounds, and natural curiosities that enable us to do far more than read the spread sheets with the members of the Finance Council. We are disciples, which is to say that we not only have various backgrounds, but we are lifelong learners; we lead rich lives that enrich others and promote the reign of God.

The Church offers us many opportunities for ongoing formation—sabbaticals, workshops, graduate education—and we should take advantage of these. But as disciples we have not only theological and pastoral interests that enrich us and our lives, but other interests too. These interests that engage us might also engage the men and women we prepare for marriage, the people we meet on sick calls, or those we come in contact with in the businesses and public institutions in the communities we serve as priests. We have hobbies and interests that delight us and offer us healthy distraction from the work of ministry, but that also find a place in our homilies and in our conversations. Our expression of these avocations can help others to see their own interests and talents not just as givens in their lives, or simply as compatible with Gospel living, but as gifts to be used in their lives of faith, too.

Priesthood can be a vital way of life, but it's not just reading theology, Scripture commentaries, or pastoral journals that enrich our lives and our ministry. So do the theater, museums, travel, reading, friends within and beyond the Church, skiing, playing the piano, or singing in the local choral society. Such things can expand our horizons and give us an ever expanding context from which to proclaim the Gospel.

We can also advance our own formation—and, at the same time, contribute to solidarity in the Church—by continuing to participate in small Christian communities like this one. A small community of priests can provide fraternity that may be scarce in

> "Ongoing formation helps the priest to overcome the temptation to reduce his ministry to an activism which becomes an end in itself, to the provision of impersonal services, even if these are spiritual or sacred, or to a businesslike function which he carries out for the Church. Only ongoing formation enables the priest to safeguard with vigilant love the 'mystery' which he bears within his heart for the good of the Church and of mankind."
>
> —Pope John Paul II
> *Pastores Dabo Vobis, § 72*

"Nothing is more practical than finding God,
that is, than falling in love in a quite absolute, final way.

What you are in love with, what seizes your imagination,
will affect everything.

It will decide what will get you out of bed in the morning,
what you do with your evenings,
how to spend your weekends,
what you read,
who you know,
what breaks your heart,
and amazes you with joy and gratitude.

Fall in love, stay in love
and it will decide everything."

**Prayer attributed to
Father Pedro Arrupe SJ, (1907-1991)
28th Superior General
of the Society of Jesus**

an era of one-priest rectories; groups that include lay men and women can contribute to our own formation and spiritual renewal and to our deeper understanding of the people to whom we minister. For everyone, these groups provide an opportunity to deepen their faith and connect it to their everyday lives. There are five essential elements to a small Christian community: prayer, both in and beyond the group; faith sharing about one's relationship with God or a connection between a Scripture passage and one's personal experience; mutual support among the members as they come to know each other's needs and concerns; learning from each other and from reading and reflecting on Scripture; and action out in the world as a personal response to the word and the sharing in the group. Faith sharing and learning may take place mostly during the group's meetings; prayer, mutual support, and action have implications for the participants' lives beyond the meetings. In fact, all five elements become a way of life.

## CONVERSATION

As we approach the end of these sessions, let's take a moment to consider these questions:

- How have you either come to discover and or to more deeply appreciate some real opportunities for lifelong learning in your life as a man and as a priest?

- How have you seen these interests, gifts and talents enrich your life and, perhaps, your priestly ministry too?

■ What are some of the things that intrigue you, that, with some encouragement, might become an occasion for ongoing learning or enrichment?

# MISSION

*Jesus emphasized the connection between faith and action, between what we believe and what we do. In that spirit, decide on an individual or group action that flows from what you have talked about in this session. If you decide to act on your own, share your decision with the group. If you decide on a group action, determine among you whether individual members will take responsibility for various aspects of the action.*

"Today, perhaps more than ever before, it is important to recognize that learning is a lifelong experience. Rapid, radical changes in contemporary society demand well-planned, continuing efforts to assimilate new data, new insights, new modes of thinking and acting."

**To Teach as Jesus Did: A Pastoral Message on Catholic Education, § 43, USCCB**

*You are likely to benefit most from taking an action that arises from your own response to the session. However, if you don't sense God asking something specific of you, you can consider one of the following suggestions or use these ideas to help develop one of your own:*

■ If you have been putting off pursuing a hobby or an intellectual interest or a form of recreation, act on it now.

■ Enroll in a course on leadership or management.

■ Enroll in a course that will introduce you to a new subject—in history, science, or music, for example—or that will expand your knowledge in a field you already know.

■ Take steps to continue meeting with your fellow priests in a small Christian community. Consider using *PRAYERTIME* from RENEW International as a resource for your group. *PRAYERTIME* uses the Sunday Gospels as the focal point for reflection, faith-sharing, and commitment to action (see page 112 for details).

■ Listen to Father Richard Chiola's reflection on lifelong learning in the audio book *Renewing the Priestly Heart* from RENEW International (see details at back of book).

■ Consider reading the complete book *Priests for the Third Millennium* by Archbishop Timothy M. Dolan, which was the inspiration for *Renewing the Priestly Heart*. You might also like to read Archbishop Dolan's book *To Whom Shall We Go*, in which he explores spiritual messages drawn from the life of St. Peter, and *Doers of the Word: Putting Your Faith into Practice*, in which he writes about finding God in the ups and downs of everyday life. All of these books are published by *Our Sunday Visitor*.

## CLOSING PRAYER

*Facilitator:* Almighty God, we thank you for the time we have spent together in this community. Through our reflections on our vocation as priests, we hope to be renewed in our commitment and revitalized in our actions on behalf of your people.

*All:* **Come then, Lord my God,**
**teach my heart where**
**and how to seek you,**
**where and how to find you.**
**Lord, you are my God and my Lord,**
**and never have I seen you.**

**You have created me and recreated me**
**and you have given me**
**all the good things I possess,**

**and still I do not know you.
I was made in order to see you,
and I have not yet accomplished
what I was made for.
Look upon us, Lord;
hear us, enlighten us,
show yourself to us.
Teach me to seek you,
and reveal yourself to me as I seek,
because I can neither seek you
if you do not teach me how,
nor find you unless you reveal yourself.
Let me seek you in desiring you;
let me desire you in seeking you;
let me find you in loving you;
let me love you in finding you.**

Adapted from a prayer by St. Anselm of Canterbury

*Facilitator:* Let us offer each other a sign of peace.

*Members of the group exchange a sign of God's peace.*

*Facilitator:* Let us pray.

**All: Lord Jesus Christ, be with us as we go in
peace to love you and serve you in your
Church. Amen.**

# APPENDIX I

*LECTIO DIVINA* AND HOMILY PREPARATION

By Father Edward J. Griswold

Effective preachers develop and sustain a love for Sacred Scripture. They allow the sacred texts to have a formative influence on their communities and on their own spiritual journeys. In *Priest as Poet*, Karl Rahner states that priests must allow God's word "to absorb and subject to itself the life of the priestly individual." Christian preachers should expect both comfort and challenge from the Sacred Scriptures that they love.

Nourishing this love requires both time and conscious effort. It does not evolve automatically. Over the centuries, Christians have turned to various ascetical disciplines to enhance their love for the word of God. A recent, promising development in the life of the Church is a renewed interest in the ancient practice of *Lectio Divina*, a Benedictine discipline for reading and internalizing the Scriptures. In September 2005, Pope Benedict XVI said, "I would like in particular to recall and recommend the ancient tradition of *Lectio Divina* … If it is effectively promoted, this practice will bring to the Church—I am convinced of it—a new spiritual springtime."

The following is an explanation of how we can use *Lectio* in the preparation of our homilies. We will begin with the *Lectio* process itself, and then consider its application to homily preparation.

## THE STAGES OF *LECTIO DIVINA*

### STAGE ONE: *LECTIO*—READING

After choosing the time, place and text for our *Lectio*, we prepare ourselves for prayer by assuming a comfortable position and by quieting ourselves. Next we pray to the Holy Spirit for illumination. Only after proper preparation do we take the first step, reading (*lectio*). In *Accepting the Embrace of God*, Luke Dysinger writes, "Some Christians focus for a few moments on their breathing; others have a beloved 'prayer word' or 'prayer phrase' they gently recite in order to become interiorly silent … Use whatever method is best for you and allow yourself to enjoy silence for a few moments."

Next we read and re-read the scriptural texts as often as we like, leaving time between readings. We read slowly and calmly. In the reading, we listen so that we might hear the voice of God. We focus on the message that God wishes to communicate to us in the scriptural word. We stop at any word or phrase that touches us. We do not expect dramatic experiences. Usually God gently invites us into a deeper relationship. God teaches us to listen and to seek in silence.

When we hear and understand the scriptural texts in faith and are open to them, we hear more than human words. The Spirit speaks to us. Often the texts have a meaning that we have never previously discovered.

## STAGE TWO: *MEDITATIO*—MEDITATION

The second stage of *Lectio* is commonly referred to as meditation. Because of its diverse meanings, the word "meditation" can lead to confusion. For some it refers to a technique of thinking about or imagining a scriptural scene or verse. Here our meditation seeks the deeper meaning that lies beneath the text. Others think of meditation as a means of achieving transcendence that brings inner peace and relieves stress. Basil Pennington proposes that in *Lectio* meditation is best identified with how the Christian community understood the word in the first millennium of Christianity.

The word "ruminatio" appears frequently in early texts to explain meditation. William of St. Thierry writes: "Some part of your daily reading should each day be stored in the stomach (i.e. the memory) and be allowed to be digested. At times it should be brought up for frequent rumination." Ultimately, through our meditation, we become intimately involved with the scriptural text. We dwell on each word and appreciate its full meaning. This inner "rumination" invites us into a dialogue with God. It invites us into prayer.

## STAGE THREE: *ORATIO*—PRAYER

As a result of our meditation, we find ourselves naturally moved to prayer: adoration, contrition, thanksgiving, and petition. We use words, ideas, images or all three. We talk with God as we would with someone who loves and accepts us. In prayer, we give to God what we have discovered in ourselves through meditation.

God wants to be united with us always. In this stage of *Lectio*, we engage God in the dialogue of prayer. We both speak and listen. What we say to God out of our meditation often returns to us as the answer to our prayer. We become the listener and experience the living, transforming word that God speaks.

### STAGE FOUR: *CONTEMPLATIO*—CONTEMPLATION

As Christians, we are temples of the New Covenant. For us contemplation means to abide intimately with the God who is within. We become a space marked out for God. We begin to live our lives sacramentally. We allow God to become fixed in all that we are and all that we do.

Unfortunately, the word "contemplation," like "meditation," can cause confusion for many people. Because of the extraordinary experiences and unusual terminology associated with contemplation, there is a danger that it may seem disconnected from ordinary life. In the incarnation of Jesus, our God has become "ordinary." God is not confined to monastic enclosures or particular lifestyles. Sincere contemplation opens us to God's call to become more loving, whatever our walk of life may be.

# *LECTIO* IN HOMILY PREPARATION

Now let's consider a step-by-step procedure for using *Lectio* in preparing our homilies. This procedure is a distillation of the work of Redemptorist Father James A. Wallace (*Preaching to the Hungers of the Heart*) and Dominican Sister Margaret Mary Pazdan (*A Dominican Hermeneutical Process for Preaching Preparation*).

Initially, we should choose a time of day and a place for *Lectio* that would ensure a prayerful atmosphere. Remember that the process does not require rigid observance of structure and that it often extends beyond one sitting. We should read each of the assigned *Lectionary* texts slowly and aloud. Then choose which text or texts we wish to pray over with *Lectio*. It is suggested that for best results we pray over only one text at a time.

### *LECTIO* (READING):

- Read the text aloud and slowly at least three times.

- What word, phrase, or image captures your attention? Keep it in mind.

## *MEDITATIO* (MEDITATION):

- Stay with the word, phrase, or image that captured your attention.
- Keep repeating it.
- Become aware of what thoughts or feelings it awakens in you.
- Write down what it says to you and how you might respond.
- Make your written response as tangible and specific as possible.
- Read over what you have written. Is there something missing?

## *ORATIO* (PRAYER) AND *CONTEMPLATIO* (CONTEMPLATION):

- Pray over what God has said to you in meditation.
- Dialogue with God about your response.
- If you receive the gift of contemplation, rest in the silence.
- Listen for God to speak further to your heart.

## *STUDEO* (STUDY):

- Turn now to scriptural commentaries for a fuller understanding of the text.
- Take into account the contributions of biblical scholars.

## *LUDO* (PLAY):

- "Play" with the text by seeing how to draw out its meaning.
- Let your imagination interpret the text in ways that will connect with people's lives today.

## *PRAEDICO* (PREACH):

- Choose the central theme and goal of your preaching.

- Consult homily services for images or stories that will enrich the preaching.

- Develop the homily.

- Practice. Practice. Practice.

- Preach with passion and love for God's Word!

Father Edward J. Griswold is dean of students and director of pastoral formation at St. Mary's Seminary and University, Baltimore, MD.

# APPENDIX II

## SMALL CHRISTIAN COMMUNITIES

Many people who have been in RENEW faith-sharing groups continue to meet on a regular basis. Through their desire to grow spiritually and the commitments they make to one another, they become continuing SCCs. The remarkable growth of small groups and communities in our time, and the highly positive diocesan evaluations of RENEW small groups in terms of the spiritual growth of parishioners, motivate us to encourage and expand this type of vibrant faith experience.

We envision SCCs as part of the larger parish, indeed of the whole Catholic Church, the people of God, its tradition, teaching, leadership, and guidance. These parish-based communities exist in relationship to the authority of the local pastor and bishop, and they benefit from their role in the larger Catholic Church by living the life of the Spirit.

To realize this vision, the pastor and staff need to give priority to it. With so much else going on, they need to discern and select outstanding leadership for their SCCs, give moral support and encouragement, and entrust the leaders with the implementation of the vision.

While speaking of the value of SCCs, we do not intend to make that value exclusive or to devalue other experiences. No dynamic in and of itself can renew the church. Ultimately, it is the Spirit of God who renews the church. Yet we believe that the recent increase of small communities is one of the more significant events of our age to encourage the renewal of the church and the transformation of the world.

Ultimately, community is a gift. It is not human effort that will build SCCs. It is the Spirit of God working in and through all of us who will set hearts aflame and bring us into communion with one another, with all creation, and with God.

The love of Christ impels us (see 2 Corinthians 5:14).

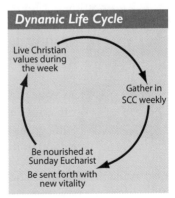

**Dynamic Life Cycle**

Live Christian values during the week

Gather in SCC weekly

Be nourished at Sunday Eucharist

Be sent forth with new vitality

### PRAYERTIME Cycle A, B, C: Faith-Sharing Reflections on the Sunday Gospels

Keep your small group gathering any time during the year with reflections on the Sunday Gospels. PRAYERTIME proposes meaningful meditations, focused faith-sharing questions, and prayers as a source of spiritual nourishment and inspiration.

PRAYERTIME is ideal for beginning meetings of the pastoral council, staff, and other parish groups. The themes can also be a useful tool for homily preparation.

This invaluable resource is also available in Spanish:

**OREMOS Ciclo A, B, C**
**Reflexiones sobre los Evangelios**
**Domincales para Compartir la Fe**

### Sowing Seeds: Essentials for Small Community Leaders

Pope John Paul II suggested considering the parish as "a community of communities." This resource draws on RENEW International's three decades of experience to offer pastoral insights and practical tips to build and expand the reach of your small Christian communities in your parish. *Sowing Seeds* overflows with simple, yet effective, ideas and strategies to communicate with your groups and enhance the way they reflect on and respond to the Gospel.

Also available in Spanish: **Sembradores de semillas: Guía para los animadores de pequeñas comunidades cristianas**

## LONGING FOR THE HOLY:
### Spirituality for Everyday Life
*Based on selected insights of Ronald Rolheiser, OMI*

Experience how the gentle spiritual guidance and practical wisdom of Catholic priest and best-selling author Fr. Ronald Rolheiser, OMI, can enliven everyday life. Suitable for small community faith sharing or individual reflection, *Longing for the Holy* covers different dimensions of contemporary spiritual life.

The *Participant's Book* contains twelve sessions with prayers, reflections, sharing questions, and stories from saints and contemporary people of faith.

This resource is also available as a four CD-set audio edition, which has both narrated text and songs for all twelve sessions.

The songs suggested for the moments of prayer in the faith-sharing sessions are offered on this 13-song anthology CD.

The kit includes the essential ingredients to bring this engaging spiritual experience to your parish or small Christian community. Purchase of the kit provides membership benefits including the opportunity for web-based workshops and faith-enrichment experiences, as well as a web library of support materials.

For more information, please visit www.renewintl.org/longing

Our complementary resource in Spanish: **Sedientos de Dios: una espiritualidad para la gente de hoy**

# SEASONAL OFFERINGS
# FROM RENEW INTERNATIONAL

### Lenten Longings, Years A, B, & C

Lent invites us to a time of prayer, reflection, and conversion. Make a six-week retreat by exploring the Sunday readings of Lent and steep yourself in the season's promptings to surrender self, work for justice, and deepen prayer life.

*Lenten Longings* is well suited for seasonal groups, small Christian communities, and individual reflection. By Catherine T. Nerney, S.S.J., Ph.D.

- ***Let Yourself Be ...*** —Year A

- ***For the Life of the World***—Year B

- ***Seeing with God's Eyes***—Year C

Companion music CD and prayer bookmark, as well as free downloadable parish resources are also available.

Our Lenten resource in Spanish:
   ***Reflexiones en Cuaresma Años A, B, & C***

### Advent Awakenings, Years A, B, & C

Advent is a time of spiritual anticipation amidst the often distracting preparations for Christmas. *Advent Awakenings*, a four-session faith-sharing experience grounded in the Sunday gospel readings, focuses on the significance of this holy season.

Appropriate for seasonal groups, small Christian communities, and individual reflection and prayer.

- ■ ***Trust the Lord***—Year A

- ■ ***Take the Time***—Year B

- ■ ***Say Yes to God***—Year C

A companion music CD and free downloadable parish resources are also available.

Our Advent resource in Spanish: ***Reflexiones en Adviento Años A, B, & C***

### Scenes from a Parish
*Special Edition DVD and Film*
*Faith-Sharing Guides*

*In English and Spanish*

Offer your parishioners a rare glimpse into one parish's real-world experience as it struggles to reconcile ideals of faith with the realities of today's changing and diverse culture.

View, reflect upon, and share faith with this special edition film and Faith-Sharing Guide and its important themes of welcoming the stranger, offering compassion, and feeding the hungry.

Ideal for parish-wide, small group, and personal viewing and reflection.

Small group sets in English or Spanish are also available.

For more information, visit: www.renewintl.org/scenes

## *Priests for the Third Millennium*

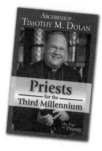

This top-selling book by Archbishop Timothy Dolan provides the basis for many of the important insights woven throughout *Renewing the Priestly Heart*.

Archbishop Dolan emphasizes true priest identity by presenting a life worth living, a life worth sharing, a life worth offering up to the Father through Christ and in the Holy Spirit.

Pastoral, practical, and thoroughly Catholic, *Priests for the Third Millennium* will renew the joy of being Catholic in the heart of seminarians, priests, and the people they serve.

Available at www.renewintl.org/priestlyheart or call 1-888-433-3221.

## *To Whom Shall We Go?*
## *Lessons from the Apostle Peter*

To be a Christian today, to follow Our Lord and accept His call to

discipleship, demands heroic courage. It takes deep faith to live the particular—special, unique—vocation that's yours alone. Heaven knows it isn't easy.

*To Whom Shall We Go?* presents the words and actions of St. Peter as it clearly shows how his life—his strengths, weaknesses, joys, and sorrows —offers an example for all of us. How it offers hope for each of us.

For this and other fine publications by Archbishop Dolan from Our Sunday Visitor, please order at www.osv.com or call 1-800-348-2440

# NOTES

# NOTES

# NOTES

# NOTES

# NOTES

# NOTES

# NOTES

# NOTES

# NOTES

# RENEWING THE PRIESTLY HEART

SPECIAL AUDIO EDITION

## The Perfect Companion for Your Spiritual Journey!

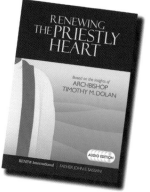

**Renewing a Priestly Heart: Special Audio Edition** is two valuable resources in a multi-CD collection. First, explore important themes related to living the priestly life today with audio reflections by nationally-known priests, a bishop, and religious. With thirteen inspiring commentaries and first-hand stories, this compilation will prompt your own spiritual renewal.

Also on CD, the full narrated text of the participant book offers a convenient format for listening at home or on the go.

**Use promo code RPH5AB for $5 off this Special Audio Edition.**

Order from our secure online bookstore at
**www.renewintl.org/priestlyheart**
or by phone at 1-888-433-3221.

# *Did you know…?*

**RENEW International** is a not-for-profit Catholic ministry organization that has touched the lives of 25 million people in the United States and 23 other countries.

From the inner city and rural areas to remote parts of the developing world, RENEW International's priority is to serve all parishes who desire to renew their faith and build the Church, regardless of their economic situation.

Throughout RENEW's dynamic history, individuals have generously reached out to support our mission.

Please join us by making a donation to RENEW International at **www.renewintl.org/donate**

## *Interested in learning more about RENEW?*

*World RENEW,* our free e-newsletter, covers interesting topics on today's spiritual life with behind-the-scenes stories and special features on RENEW International's work with parishes and small communities around the world.

To read more and explore how you can be an integral part of the RENEW International family, please return this card or visit **www.renewintl.org/subscribe**

❏ I would like to receive free *World RENEW* e-newsletters via **email.**

❏ I would like to receive a catalog and more information on other fine faith-sharing resources from RENEW International.

❏ I would like to receive information about ways to support RENEW's mission.

Title (Circle one)   Ms.   Mrs.   Mr.   Sr.   Br.   Fr.
Other, please specify: _____

Name _____

Address _____

_____

Phone _____

Email _____
*Required for your email subscription. Your email will not be shared with other parties.*

SS2011